D0759968

BIOSPHERES

also by the author

MICROCOSMOS

GARDEN OF MICROBIAL DELIGHTS

ORIGINS OF SEX

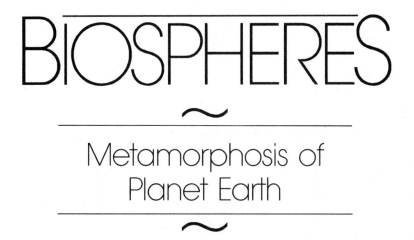

BIOSPHERES

~

Metamorphosis of Planet Earth

~

by
DORION SAGAN

McGRAW-HILL PUBLISHING COMPANY

New York   St. Louis   San Francisco
Toronto   Hamburg   Mexico

1 2 3 4 5 6 7 8 9 DOC DOC 9 5 4 3 2 1 0

ISBN 0-07-054426-3

Library of Congress Cataloging-in-Publication Data

Sagan, Dorion.
  Biospheres : metamorphosis of planet earth / Dorion Sagan.
    p. cm.
  Bibliography: p.
  Includes index.
  ISBN 0-07-054426-3
  1. Biosphere. I. Title.
QH313.S24 1989
575'.001—dc19   89-2680
                                                                    CIP

Book design by Eve Kirch

CONTENTS

EARTH

Yes, happily language is a thing: it is a written thing, a bit of bark, a sliver of rock, a fragment of clay in which the reality of the earth continues to exist.

—Maurice Blanchot

Introduction

Science-fiction stories have depicted parallel worlds inhabited by various types of individuals: persons evolving beyond flesh into a state of pure information; space-faring mutants who have forgotten their own earthly origins; and humans merging with extraterrestrial beings. In science fiction, the moon, then Mars, the moons of Jupiter and Saturn, and finally the entire solar system become settled by human life as planet Earth once was settled by bacteria, plants, fungi, and animals. In science fiction, technology becomes so complex, miniaturized, and advanced that its effects are indistinguishable from magic. In science fiction, computers and robots become intelligent, sentient entities—the mechanical, silicon-based offspring of carbon-based life.

But this book is not about science fiction. It is about reality.

The central tenet of this book is that we live in a world more exciting than any invented by science fiction. If we take a careful, philosophical look at ourselves, we find that many of the scenarios dreamed up by science fiction are already occurring, have already occurred, or are bound to occur.

My hope is that, after a philosophical excursion into the nature of life, you come away with the realization that the Earth is not only living but alive. Far from being an inert lump of matter, the Earth behaves as a giant organism. In this book I move beyond James Lovelock's increas-

ingly scientifically accepted view that the surface of the Earth is a physiological being (which he calls "Gaia")[1] to show that it is actually on
the verge of reproduction. The best example of this is the system under
construction in the desert near Tucson, Arizona, an enclosed, luxurious, human-containing terrarium called "Biosphere II." The purpose of
this structure is to house plants, animals, and microbes in such a way
that people can dwell independently from humanity's original home—
which in retrospect becomes "Biosphere I."[2] Praising a building, sixteenth-
century Italian painter Giorgio Vasari wrote that it appeared "not built,
but born."[3] From one point of view, the human-containing terraquariums
known as biospheres are merely ambitious examples of intelligent architecture and engineering. But from another, more global, perspective they
are the products of a life bent on making more of itself: they, too, are not
built, but born.

   Not only is the Earth already beginning the process of reproducing
itself, but the presence of life anywhere in the universe is a signal that
the whole of reality is, in a sense, alive. Although there is little scientific
evidence to support this view of universal life, Aristotle and other Greek
philosophers who laid the metaphysical foundations for Western science,
held similar views. In addition, some thinkers at the forefront of quantum
mechanics, such as physicist David Bohm, believe that the mechanical
world view is no longer supportable and that the universe (physical reality
from the level of quarks to galaxies) displays features of wholeness that
make it far more like an *organism*, an integral entity, than any collection
of essentially unrelated atoms or parts.

   The Gaia hypothesis holds that environmental variables at the surface
of the Earth (such as the salinity and acid-base balance of the oceans and
the carbon dioxide and oxygen levels of the atmosphere) are controlled
precisely by the sum of planetary life. This hypothesis has not yet been
proven to the satisfaction of many scientists; yet, as I show later in this
book, the idea that the Earth is alive is not so much an hypothesis as a
world view—a way of looking at things that can produce not only testable
scientific hypotheses but also a fresh understanding of what humankind
means to the future of planetary life. The step from one world view to
another is over a yawning abyss, and my game in *Biospheres* has been to
make this jump while looking down. In the end, the planet, like the
universe, may be neither alive nor a vast mechanism but it is, to paraphrase
J. B. S. Haldane, "queerer than we can imagine." Understanding the
way in which the Earth is using people to reproduce itself makes for a

story more real and yet more unbelievable than the strangest science fiction.

According to the Committee on Planetary Biology of the National Research Council, endorsed by the National Academy of Sciences, the biosphere is "the large-scale planetary system that includes, sustains, and is influenced by life."[4] The United States National Commission on Space, directed by Thomas Paine, reported on the future of space, saying in part:

A biosphere is an enclosed ecological system. It is a complex, evolving system within which flora and fauna support and maintain themselves and renew their species, consuming energy in the process. A biosphere is not necessarily stable; it may require intelligent tending to maintain species at the desired levels. Earth supports a biosphere; up to now we know of no other examples. To explore and settle the inner Solar System, we must develop biospheres of smaller size, and learn how to build and maintain them.[5]

Biosphere II grabs our attention because it is the most ambitious attempt to date to form a closed ecosystem, and it seems to be a necessary intermediate step in preparation for living in space. We might compare the attempt to build a perpetually recycling biosphere that houses human beings to epic endeavors in the past, such as humanity's freeing itself from the embrace of gravity, epitomized by the flight of the Wright brothers and by the Apollo craft landing on the moon. But despite the majestic symbolism of Biosphere II—building another Earth—we immediately notice a difference between it and these other technological triumphs: both the attempt to fly and the moon shot were discrete: they were definitively accomplished. The Apollo program has even been criticized for being too discrete, too final: after the political goal of beating the Soviets in a space race was accomplished, nothing was left to be done. All seemed anticlimactic. Biosphere II won't have this problem. Indeed, its success will be defined negatively, as an absence of failure. What is definitive success? Eight people living inside it for two years? How about ten years, or a century? In fact, biosphere production, the building of dwellings that internally recycle all that is needed for human life, begins something whose end we cannot foresee. It inaugurates the participation of humankind and, more importantly, of life on Earth as a whole in the destiny of the universe.

The Wright brothers, the later successful development of hang gliders, and the aerodynamic machines that were unsuccessfully implemented during the Renaissance manifested the ancient dream of human flight. It is difficult, on the other hand, to imagine early humans dreaming of creating materially closed ecosystems; this is a new quest. Regardless of the relative success or failure of Biosphere II, the mere undertaking of such a project, its very presence, reminds us of something else. We are in the midst of an event, an unfolding far greater than a local construction project. Whether or not Biosphere II succeeds in supporting human beings indefinitely or degrades into a giant algal heap, biospheres themselves are destined to arrive; there is about them an air of evolutionary inevitability.

From an evolutionary perspective Biosphere II,[6] the Soviet Bios projects,[7] test-tube-size ecosystems,[8] and other efforts[9] testify to the budding, the first tentative reproducing, of planet Earth as a biological identity. We are at the first phase of a planetary metamorphosis, a breaking of the biontic wave. By "biontic" I refer to a biont, a biological unit; by "wave" I mean the cresting and reappearance of individuality at a hitherto unsuspected scale: not of reproducing microorganisms, or plants or animals, but of the Earth as a living whole. Over evolutionary time we see the formation of new biological units at ever more inclusive levels of integration. We know about reproduction: cells reproduce, and those multicellular collections of cells—plants and animals—reproduce. But now we see on the horizon the first reproduction of ecosystems as discrete, semi-independent units. Yes, human beings are involved in this reproduction, but are not insects involved in the reproduction of many flowers? That the living Earth now depends upon us and our engineering technology for its reproduction does not invalidate the proposition that biospheres, ostensibly built for the convenience of human beings, represent the reproduction of the planetary biosystem. Biospheres are new, both in the limited realm of human architecture and technology and in the larger domain of Earth history. Biospheres announce the beginnings of a new eon. In geological terminology, eons extend about 1000 million years. Biospheres signal a new eon beyond the Phanerozoic Eon geologists describe as our current one. They signal the differentiation and networking—the blastulation—of life before it moves into space. (A "blastula" is an early, spherical stage in the formation of animal embryos.)

The reproduction of the Earth is a major focus of this book. Another focal point is a prognostication, a prediction, about the future that I hope is wrong even as I fear it is correct. This prediction concerns the technological metamorphosis of the planet itself, a breakup or differentiation of the Earth's surface into separately functioning ecosystems—isolated enclaves, each with their own inhabitants: human, technological, and botanical. I think we tend to underestimate the extent to which biospheres will be formed on Earth rather than in space. Physicist Philip Morrison from the Massachusetts Institute of Technology suggests that the next logical place for human habitation is the oceans; settling the oceans would be far cheaper than living in space. Recycling systems could allow people to live on top of or underneath the oceans—to bring the environment of land to the water in a reversal of the ancient process by which life encapsulated the wet environment of the oceans in the waxy cuticle of plants and in the shells and skin of land animals. The evolution of plants depended on the formation of a protective water-retentive outer coating by colonies of algal cells. Submarine cities, in turn, will depend upon the formation of air-retentive enclosures by colonies of much larger organisms.

This settling of the subocean and of intra-, as opposed to extraterrestrial, space may be a positive development, a luxurious expanding of the space available for human living. On the other hand, the breakup of the Earth could be precipitated by the inevitabilities of overcrowding and worldwide pollution. The surface of the Earth may become a kaleidoscopic, multiform copy of itself, not because a few people desire it but because of lack of alternatives. A disturbing possibility is that future life may exist only inside ecological enclosures, each a kind of biologically miniaturized world. Seen from afar, the compartmentalization of environments at the surface of the Earth would look blastospheric—like an embryo in an early stage of its differentiation.

In his famous paper *Tragedy of the Commons*, biologist Garrett Hardin shows how, in pursuit of individual gain, sheep owners do not restrain their sheep from overgrazing common ground. As everyone exploits the commons, the pasture is ruined.[10] So it is with us. As individual people and nation states fail to restrain themselves from pursuing selfish advantage—maximizing individual wealth and national gross product—we begin to share in the tragic deterioration of our own pasture: the global commons of atmosphere and oceans. Not only is the supply of wool sweaters and of mutton threatened but also human being itself. An article in *Science News* suggests that the correlation between carbon dioxide increase and human population has been so close over the last twenty-five years that the census might be better taken by atmospheric measure-

ment of this waste gas.[11] The irony is that as ecologists race to meetings
or inaugurate letter-writing campaigns to save the rainforest, they drive
or fly to their destinations, use paper products, add fossil fuel exhaust to
the atmosphere exacerbating the greenhouse effect, and eat beef from
cattle raised by clearing forests, thus adding to the very problems that
worry them. I even feel a little uncomfortable using reams of paper to
write and rewrite my speculations on the future transformation of the
biosphere.

As human populations grew in the past, the shared lands of indige-
nous peoples gave way to the partitioned lots of landlords and polities;
land ownership and national boundaries replaced open territory. I foresee
an analogous development with biospheres in the future. As three-
dimensional property encompassing the atmosphere once thought to belong to no one, biospheres will ensure their sequestered inhabitants clean
air, fresh water, and edible food. In the highly populated, polluted world
of the future, biospheres, part of the living architecture of the Earth itself,
will not be isolated academic or experimental laboratories. Although certainly there are many ways in which decentralized local ecologies would
benefit people and would improve our relationship with nature, greed
has not yet been weaned out of human beings. Rapacious plunderers—
polluting companies, their stockholders, and powerful, resource-draining
nations—who enrich themselves at the expense of others are not punished;
indeed, in today's world they are materially rewarded for their vice. The
ultimate result of entrenched selfishness is a globally deteriorating environment. The only way to avert polluting the oceanic, atmospheric, near
space, electromagnetic, and other commons is for the members of human
nations to realize and behave as integral parts of a single collective entity
or organism. Even if we don't recognize our planetary interrelatedness,
it remains true that our destinies are fused and that we will live or die
together, integrated, perhaps, into the life cycle of a single giant being.

At first glance, biosphere production—the creation of enclosed, ecologically sustaining territories—appears to be a technological, cultural,
and human process. In fact, however, artificial biospheres are not artificial
at all. Biosphere production mirrors previous developments in evolutionary history. About 2 billion years ago certain cells, known in their fossil
form as acritarchs, were preserved in the fossil record. These cells went
into a phase of their life cycle resistant to death by radiation or desiccation.
Purely biological structures such as bacterial cysts, fungal spores, the seeds
of flowers, and the eggs of birds and reptiles are also phases of the life

cycle resistant to radiation and desiccation. Properly speaking, they are propagules. Recent scholarship suggests that the ancient Egyptian Pharaohs believed that, by copying on a grand scale the burying antics of the scarab beetle, they could preserve their living essence underground in mummy-wrapped sarcophagi inside pyramids and be reborn in the life to come. [12] Indeed, the royal provisioning of wealth as gold jewels and foods in a subterranean Egyptian space resembles not only the life cycle of dung beetles but also nature's formation of seedlike propagule structures in general.

The "man-made" ecosystems known as biospheres are ultimately "natural"—a planetary phenomenon that is part of the reproductive antics of life as a whole. Biospheres recall but transcend past developments in life's history. Merging ecology and technology, they contain life in seed form. This seed form can, with suitable evolutionary and technological advances, protect and disseminate Earth life across the Milky Way galaxy. Humankind has been drawn into the ancient biological tradition of forming enclosed protective structures that endure environmental hardships not withstood by other forms. We can no longer afford to see ourselves as superior. We do not stand at the summit of terrestrial nature; we are not above life but inside it. Indeed, though it sounds comical, we are part of the "genitals" of Earth life, the planetary counterpart to reproductive organs. We will have been crucial to the birth of Earth's first batch of cosmic young.

The desire to get off the Earth and live in space has been called a modern religion. But with biospheres we see how such living in space will be done. For the first time we recognize our cosmic role as midwives aiding in the gestation, delivery, and development of a new form of life. Combined with astronautics, biospheric life is uniquely fit to preserve and spread our earthly heritage even after the death of the sun. Arising from Mother Earth we find ourselves incestuously involved in her reproduction. As a technological species we have initiated a process of imitation that copies not a gene or an organism but planetary life as a unified ecological system. This copying process does not belong to the distant future or another dimension but to this very world. As such, it is more real than anything to be found in science fiction. The projected change of the living Earth is as astounding—and yet, as natural—as the transformation of a crawling insect into a flying one. It is nothing less than the metamorphosis of planet Earth.

AIR

It is something to be able to paint a particular picture, or to carve a statue, and so to make a few objects beautiful; but it is far more glorious to carve and paint the very atmosphere and medium through which we look, which morally we can do. To affect the quality of the day, that is the highest of the arts.

—Henry David Thoreau

CHAPTER 1

~

Beyond Humanity

When I write of the metamorphosis of planet Earth I do not mean it only in the grand sense of biosphere production, of reproduction on a global scale, or of the end of a human era and the beginning of a planetary one. I also use the phrase to refer to the literal transformation of the substance of the Earth into these pages. The pen I use to write belongs not to me but to the Earth, to the Earth writing a note to itself. The pen is not just a felt-tip marker but extends from my writing hand to my whole body and brain: I am an instrument in the play of Earth. Indeed, etymologically, this is not pure fantasy: the word "organism" comes from *órganon*, Greek for instrument. Not only in my mind but within a certain symbolism, I am part of the Earth, remarking, inscribing, scarring, and scaring itself.

British atmospheric chemist James Lovelock, who has developed and supported the Gaia hypothesis, which holds that the Earth regulates itself as if it were a giant living organism, compares the live Earth to a tree. Planet Earth, like a California redwood tree, is mostly dead. Yet as a whole—like the redwood tree—it lives. On a tree, only a ring of cells near the circumference grows. So, too, eon by eon part of Earth grows, moving away from the home of its origin, encroaching upon new territories, and leaving in its wake circles of dead and discarded tissue.[1] As humans we too are on the edge, the ringlike ledge spreading off the fertile surface into space. Such an analogy demonstrates a new attentiveness to

the distinction between death and life and suggests that the distinction
may not be as simple as it first appears.

In this book I question several such distinctions that we tend to take
for granted. One is the distinction between life and nonlife. Cells live;
we live; the Earth is a living planet. But the Earth's life depends upon
the sun, which is part of the solar system and the Milky Way galaxy. Are
they all living? Where do we draw the line between life and nonlife or
between an organism and the matter (food, water, air) an organism uses
to remain itself? Another is the distinction between the Earth as a mechanism and as an organism. A third is the distinction between technology
and life. I suspect that the separations effected by these distinctions may
be fabricated—illusions of language.

A focus on biospheres will allow us to discuss these distinctions, and
to look with new eyes on the familiar terrain we all too often take for
granted.[2]

Wes Jackson, an ecologically concerned plant geneticist, speaks of the
dangers of technology, especially of biotechnology, which he thinks is
moving forward far too fast for the public good ("We may be going to
Hell in a handbasket, but why motorize it?"). Jackson claims that the
Gaia hypothesis that the Earth is an organism is just poetry and, furthermore, it may be bad poetry. To prove his assertion, Jackson points
out that all organisms have offspring. For the Earth to be an organism,
there would have to be baby earths, planetary offspring. Therefore the
Earth cannot be an organism.

However, through technology and human engineering the Earth *is*
beginning to create offspring. These tiny biospheres are the closed ecological environments under construction in the United States, the Soviet
Union, Japan, and elsewhere. The biospheres are prerequisites for life in
space. These human-sized terraria—or, rather, terraquaria, because they
contain bodies of water as well—miniaturize the global ecosystem, the
single, original biosphere in which, until now, life has always dwelled.

Such systems—though ostensibly made solely for *Homo sapiens*—
represent the reproduction of the biosphere *through* human beings. Seen
from this perspective, the Earth is beginning to reproduce, which provides
clinching evidence that it is a global organism. The idea that the Earth
is alive is not bad poetry at all. It is good poetry, which does not mean

it is bad science. The amoeba is a unicellular organism; an animal is a multicellular organism; the most familiar organisms are composites with components that once lived as separate individuals. In the case of the Earth, the separate individuals coming together include the technically steeped animals so important to the functioning of the first generation of biospheres: people.

I asked Jackson how we should think of the biosphere, if not as an organism. "How should we think of God?" he asked. I didn't have an answer. I also don't have an answer as to how to think of Earth. Our minds and bodies are so complex that it is reductionist to think of ourselves solely in terms of biology. But, if we are organisms, and some cells are organisms, then the Earth, too, must be regarded in a similar vein. It is alive, not just a chemical and a physical but also a physiological and maybe even a psychological system.

Jackson suggested the problem is one of pride. There is something to be said, he remarked, for the old idea of a great hierarchy of beings, with people above—and more responsible than—other animals, yet below—and destined never to be as powerful as—the angels. Such systems can keep us humble.

But the same restrictions on arrogance can apply if we think of the Earth as alive and of ourselves doing service to that which is greater, longer-lived, and more profound. We don't need to return to the antiquated concept of a great chain of being to have humility. We can understand and rise up to the level of the Earth. Nonetheless, Jackson's point is well taken: we do not know what the Earth is.

In 1986 I was invited to visit the site of Biosphere II, a multimillion cubic-foot structure whose goal is to contain animals, plants, and microbes in a perpetually recycling ecosystem. Also inside will be "biospherians," human inhabitants caretaking an environment cut off from Mother Earth and sealed in glass and steel. With some of the men and women involved in the project I ate tilapia, freshwater fish reared in tanks that recycle fish waste into plant food. The tilapia were delicious, blackened as per Cajun recipes and served at a local restaurant. Such total recycling design can provide an endless supply of food for those inside "artificial" ecosystems.

To section ourselves off from the Earth's biosphere in order to prepare for life in space stations or upon other worlds, we must recreate the mother biosphere in miniature. We can't go alone but must take representative organisms integrated into natural ecosystems with us. If we were to set up an independent colony on Mars, we would have to recreate an Earthlike ecosystem on a smaller scale. Mars would be remade in the image of Earth. If we step out of our human-centered outlook for a moment, we see life as a multispecies phenomenon; we see that our technology guides many nonhuman species as well, establishing them, no less than us, in extraterrestrial environments. Indeed, our technology is not really our own. I am convinced that technology is part of the evolutionary process itself. Technology is *natural*.

Over time the biosphere grows, including more and more so-called inanimate matter in its metabolism. You can look at technology as the interface between the living Earth and the chemical compounds it assimilates into its metabolism. As the biosphere grows, matter literally comes to life. Such incorporation of new materials into living organization did not start with humankind but has been going on since life began over 3 billion years ago. Technology's tools and instruments transcend humanity. Evolutionarily, once life gets into space using recycling technology, it will loosen itself from the Earth and man. It will snap off the earthly umbilical cord. Although it is easy to overlook recycling technologies as but a small step in a long history of amazing feats of human engineering, this small step represents a giant leap for life as a whole. The move to space via recycling technologies announces a changeover as dramatic as the encroachment millions of years ago by the ancestors of plants (soon to be followed by animals) onto dry land.

While there is no telling what may happen, we have great hubris if we imagine future life forms in space will be dominated by humans. From afar, the tenure of life on land may look as brief as the moment an Olympic diving champion springs down upon upon the diving board before soaring into space. Although magic, animistic powers are attributed to nature in many native cultures, and although the power of animals is the focus of relationships for shamans, very few of us in modern Western society are aware of the vast influences of the nonhuman living world. We ignore entirely the likelihood that nonhuman life prompts or spurs technological humanity. Humanity is just one in thousands of species that are producing the technology necessary to differentiate and deliver life's "young." Just as the crawling fish ancestral to all amphibians no longer exists, so the human race may vanish to become but a trace. Once Earth's biosphere reproduces into biospheres, the Earth itself—our planetary parent—could be crushed like a sunflower seed with no threat of violence to life as a whole. Biospheric reproduction announces a certain maturity of life, in which life as life uses humanity to infiltrate, settle, and transform the environment of the solar system and beyond.

The rise of humanity has been in the nature of a sacrifice; it has caused the precipitous demise of many older parts of the biosphere. Today's feelings of alienation and dissatisfaction with the environmental carnage we have caused may be a hopeful sign however. Even though the greenhouse effect of planetary warming resulting from air pollution may not yet have occurred, it has entered into public dialogue as a concern about the global environment. People discuss acid rain, waste disposal, and holes in the ozone layer. The anatomy of the biosphere is being felt, becoming known.

Environmental protection, however, can never be accomplished simply by exerting goodwill. Even those vegetarians who diligently use only natural rub-on antiperspirants, who drive to ecological conferences and eat refrigerated food, accelerate the deterioration of the environment: from cars come carbon monoxide and dioxide fumes; the plastic containers of the all-natural products fall short of easy biodegradability; and refrigerators produce more fluorocarbons than deodorant sprays. Technology is here to stay. We cannot go back to nature, but only watch in stupefaction as technology weaves into, becomes part of, the living Earth as a whole.

The spread of technology alarms us; liberals and conservatives alike long to return to the green, unspoiled, pristine countryside. Strange, however, comes the realization that our tall fields of grass and rolling pastures represent precisely the death traps—the polluted live burial grounds and wastelands of other organisms who once thrived but were poisoned by oxygen. Most died, but some survived to beget us. Analogously, cities, with their soot, crowds, concrete, honking cars, and thirty-one flavors of pollution may be the bucolic paradise of our descendants. Today they foster claustrophobia and paranoia; tomorrow they may be the heart of the serene. Our discomfort with technology presumably derives from our heritage as animals of tropical forests; we are physiologically tuned to, psychologically primed for, a primary habitat that no longer exists. A science-fiction story portrays the landing of an extraterrestrial

visitor in the middle of a busy urban intersection. "What peace! What
serenity!" he exclaims. The descendants of human beings may be adapted
to precisely the "unnatural" environments that harry us now.

It would be difficult to wax poetic about medical waste, chlorofluo-
rocarbons, and carbon dioxide. Yet smog can enhance the colors of a
sunset. Excrement, garbage, trash—all the most rancid and marginal parts
of our anatomy, personal and planetary—are one day transmuted into
parrots, wine grapes, magnolia trees, into the colorful and aromatic nature
we so admire.[3] When a tumor-producing cell spreads through the lung
or skin, we say a person has cancer. Indeed, some have compared human
technological growth at the Earth's surface to a cancer or a tumor. A less
familiar interpretation is the Gaian one that the biosphere behaves as a
young superorganism. A pregnant woman shows symptoms, she undergoes
"abnormal growth," and she experiences sharp pains. Sensing itself
through us, the biosphere suffers with the weight of an urbanized world.
But, barring fatal childbirth trauma, the result may not be death so much
as new life.

The spread of our species' urban and technological havoc may represent something similar: the biosphere struggling to grow, to give birth.
Planetary sickness should end not in death but in rebirth, both of human
culture and of Earth life as an entity. From this angle, the technological
swelling and unease should be taken very seriously. We are in the presence
of something growing—something as dangerous as a tumor and as hopeful
as an embryo. And we should all be prepared. As Jackson says, we don't
know what Earth is. At a moment's notice humanity may be called upon
to perform some crucial midwifery, the cosmic equivalent of an emergency
delivery. Such an operation will be unlike anything in the history of the
human species, not because it is difficult as an engineering feat—indeed,
biospherics probably draws upon fewer technical skills than astronautics
—but because transplanting life into space begins an era for life as a
whole. Its importance transcends the human species. As an event, the
transplantation of life into space means more than the human species
itself.

Across the black rivers of space, we are the biosphere's bridges to the
stars. Certainly, the bridges seem indispensable and may be full of traffic
for a long while. Yet, once having accomplished their mission, they could
be burned or could crumble like an old footbridge in the woods without
our descendants really noticing or caring, let alone staring in wonder or
shedding a nostalgic tear.

*   *   *

A biosphere is a special kind of living system, one with enough different kinds of organisms doing different things to support life in a closed environment. A biosphere resembles an organism in that it is a fundamental unit of life. Life cannot leave Earth and settle elsewhere without forming biospheres; it cannot change without staying the same. Science-fiction writer Harlan Ellison once wrote a pilot for a TV series in which people in biospheres persisted for many generations in space and eventually lost touch with their earthly history, which lived on only as legend. The same theme was explored by Robert Heinlein in his novella *Universe*.

Logically enough (at the time there were no commercial jets), fiction written in the 1950s described the insides of space vehicles using nautical terminology, the language of boats. In fact, the insides of "ships" designed for prolonged space voyages would more likely resemble what is outside on Earth than they would the inside of a boat, an airplane, or an urban apartment. The dynamics needed to sustain life in space crucially depend on technology but primarily as a hull or hard external casing; in space, as on Earth, the real work would be done by assemblages of bacteria, algae, plants, and animals. We might be disposable—necessary only for the extraterrestrial genesis, the seeding or sowing, of Earth life. Human beings are not self-sufficient but depend on life as a system. Once life gets loose in space there is no telling what may happen, certainly no guarantee that *Homo sapiens* will stay in control. Indeed, many people today are attracted to the Fullerian idea that the Earth is a kind of spaceship, a space-faring biospheric ark with humanity at the helm. The suggestion that nonhuman life may mutiny—even in the alien environments of space, in some far-off future—some find worrisome.

But like most science-fiction scenarios, this one of mutiny really does not belong in the future as much as in the present. People are not in charge right now. For the most part, we are just a tunnel-visioned, self-serving species, highly dangerous to ourselves and to a few other species, and fascinated by the technology we imagine is our own. Such delusions of grandeur and control go hand in hand with the development of powerful technologies, but they are frills to the overall biospheric structure. We exist because other organisms cycle the biosphere with needed materials. Even without genetic engineering's promise (or threat) to redesign life, it is virtually impossible that 5 or so billion years from now there would be people whom we would recognize as such. Five billion years in the future is the time at which theories of stellar evolution predict our life-giving sun will undergo extensive nuclear reactions and expand into a red giant, perhaps even sizzling away the Earth's oceans. By that time, self-enclosed ecologically designed systems—the acronym is SEEDS—may have spread life to other planets, other solar systems, perhaps even fertilized the Milky Way into a galactic garden. Is it right to colonize other worlds? Even if it isn't, can it be stopped? The death of the sun that astronomers say will gravitationally collapse in about 5 billion years would be but one obstacle among many overcome by global life. Life would reveal itself to be not merely a planetary but a cosmic phenomenon, a phenomenon in which human beings are a surface or a mask—transitory ripples on the universal lake rather than the lake itself.

Writer Peter Corning points out that the word "biosphere" is subversive, subtly undermining nationalistic aims.[4] Mere mention of it provides a clue that our allegiance may not be to the special interests of a few but to the planetary concerns of the many. That includes not just other races but also other species. In a limited world, problems come home to roost: the ancient idea of karma resonates with this concept of an ultimately limited material economy. On Earth there is no escape, no exit, from global ecology. The concept dawns that we are citizens of the biosphere, that true patriots are patriots of Earth. But the Earth, from space, is not the static map we see in our flat books and atlases. Astronaut Eugene Cernan observed from his Earth-orbiting perspective that

> You literally see North and South America go around the corner as the Earth turns on an axis you can't see and then miraculously Australia, then Asia, then all of America comes up to replace them. You see a multicolored, three-dimensional picture of Earth. You begin to see how little we understand of time. You ask yourself the question "Where really am I in space and time?"[5]

Throughout our daily lives we move through layers of biosphere as a fish moves through the depths of a lake. The medium we do not see is not water, but air. For life to inhabit a planet, it must make use of that planet's conducting medium, the medium through which chemicals are cycled on a global scale. On Earth all we say and do occurs within such a medium. This medium is the biospheric membrane, the transparent atmosphere in which we live and breathe and which carries our voices as well as many other sounds produced and sensed by organisms in their environment.

In "Merleau-Ponty and the Voice of the Earth," by American philosopher David Abram we note the following on the possibility that language, no less than technology, is not our own but in some sense owned by and owed to the biosphere:

> If language is rooted in perception, then it is never, in actuality, a language of wholly abstract, ideal, or purely mathematical relations, for it is inhabited by all those things, styles and rhythms to which our senses give us access. Indeed, we may begin to discern that this our language has been contributed to, and is still sustained by, many gestures, expressions and sounds besides those of our single species! A language that has its real genesis in the deep world of untamed perception is a language that was born as a call for and a response to a gesturing, sounding, speaking landscape—a world of thunderous rumblings, of chattering brooks, of flapping, flying, screeching things, of roars and sighing winds. . . .[6]

That is why Merleau-Ponty could write, in his unfinished work, that "language is everything, since it is the voice of no one, since it is the very voice of the things, the waves and the forests. . . ." "We may even begin to suspect," says Abram, "that this language we speak is the voice of the living Earth itself, singing through the human form. . . . Logos is realized in us, but is is not our property."[7] The issue of property (the proper, the appropriate, the "own") is a hot topic now in European "post-modern" philosophy. What belongs to humanity? I contend that the biosphere, *through me*, may be writing or helping to write these words. But if I can say this, the very notion of an "I" separate from the biosphere comes under question.

WATER

Do not think of the water failing; for this water has no end.

—Rumi

CHAPTER 2

~

The Wave

Life is a wave. The moon pulls at the water, lifting up a blue fold in the ocean that may travel a mile or so before crashing into the shore. The matter of which a wave is made is continually rearranging—spilling over and into itself to form itself anew. Although we can follow the wave, it is never the same as it consists of completely different particles 200 yards from shore than it does when it crests.

The particles of which your body is composed also do not stay the same but are in a state of continual flux. Tracking the flow of the matter of life guarantees that now in your body are atoms that once grew in the tree of Buddha, soiled the clothes of Jesus, and reflected as the eye of Picasso. As with the continuous recycling of water in the ocean to make waves, the pool of chemical elements from which we are made is finite. Matter, especially living matter, cycles. With each breath you take, each bead of sweat that evaporates from your skin, or each scone that you consume, you replace chemical constituents in your body. In no two consecutive moments are you or any other life form composed of exactly the same particles.

Only several inches high when it sweeps across mid-ocean, a tsunami may swell up into a hundred-foot wall of water as it plunges into an island or a continental shelf, consuming land, trees, homes, and whatever else lies in its way. So, too, the wave of planetary life is greedy and indiscriminate in its use of materials. All forms of life use a certain minimal variety of chemical elements in their bodies; over time, that variety has increased. For example, at one time on the surface of the earth, free oxygen was not respired by cells, but today many cells use it: atmospheric oxygen has entered the biosphere's repertoire of circulating elements. Material existence threads through life, as saltwater weaves through a wave.

Life developed at the ocean edge, and we still have a deep, even endless connection to water. Chemically, our insides are presumably still as wet and as salty as the early oceans in which our marine ancestors evolved. Most of our weight is in the form of water. From one point of view, life on land literally represents *emergence*, that is, the rising up and spreading out of the sea. Enclosed in waterproof leaves and skin, we "terrestrial" beings bring the sea up from the depths. On Earth, the sea keeps rising. In an uncanny way, it is always high tide.

But life does not only use water in its self-organization. Instead, life straddles the line between liquid and solid, specializing in colloidal, jelly-like proteins and quivering liquids. Over time life has gravitated to still harder, more durable materials—armor and armaments to protect the soft and vulnerable essential parts. For instance, organisms use carbon, phosphorus, sulfur, and strontium in the formation of skeletons. In making itself, marine life uses hard parts. Together organisms such as diatoms and red algae, seals and clams deplete the environment of silica and carbonate, phosphate, iodine, and fluorine. Life concentrates and redistributes, moving components from undersaturated solutions. Some chemicals, like those in the spicules of glass sponges and microscopic radiolaria, are hardened and packaged around the soft tissues of life. Some life forms drain the ocean of silica to make fiery opal; others sequester sulfates into gypsum or form crystals of barite in their bodies. Living organisms concentrate massive quantities of cobalt, nickel, copper, zinc, molybdenum, chromium, iron, phosphorus, and manganese.

For eons the whole surface of our planet has been disturbed by and conformed to the spreading of a slow "wave," more subtle than a tsunami to be sure, yet, judged by the movement of the Earth's surface, far more powerful. An example of such geological movement includes several islands off the coast of Peru, which are formed by hardened droppings of sea birds. As organisms grow and are crowded together on the surface of the Earth, this matter-moving wave becomes stronger. Soviet geochemist Andrey Vitalyevich Lapo writes that "Living matter is a specific kind of rock . . . an ancient and, at the same time, an eternally young rock. A rock which creates itself and destroys itself to originate again in new generations in the innumerable forms constituting it. The Phoenix of ancient legends. . . ."[1] The animate world of scarabs and crabs, of plants and ants, grows from and returns to the "ground," which all organisms continually draw against to construct themselves. The inexhaustibility of the Earth's mineral resources owes to an original cycling economy in which all organisms participate. The Earth is so rich and resourceful that we may forget our very identity as individuals is temporary, on loan.

In a sense, the water and calcium phosphate of our flesh and bones are our own but are not owned: they are owed; they must be returned to the oceanic Earth. When we die, our accounts are settled as bodies in the soil or ashes in the air, and the materials that made us wend their way into new forms, such as cockroaches and sunflowers. We inhabit and sustain a biosphere that is literally composed of the breath and bones of all our ancestors.

Sometimes late at night I have a lucid dream—one in which I know I am dreaming; then I inevitably awake, ending the dream. Similarly, suspecting a silent symmetry in the fabric of existence, I sometimes have the sneaking suspicion that a true understanding of my wakeful, living, state will jettison me out of it. Far from conceiving death as a perfect sleep, I fear that if I die I might awake from reality into a timeless realm that is, in the beloved adjectival phrase of certain European philosophers, "already always" there. Since this realm is already "always," one has only to not fear death—that is, to die as ego—in order to enter it. Heaven is a place, David Byrne says in a song, "where nothing ever happens." Then I begin to wonder about the world as a whole: might not the present condition of humanity on this Earth be merely an epoch from which we cannot wrest ourselves free? As if the true history of humanity had been purposely forgotten? Philosopher Alan Watts writes that people fear humans will evolve, à la science fiction, into nothing but a complex of electronic traces. But Watts points out that we have nothing to fear: we are *already* a series of such electronic traces, a matrix of nerve impulses

and sensations. We must move, as R. D. Laing puts it, from the fear of
nothing to nothing to fear.

The greater our awareness becomes of our surroundings, the more
difficult it is to say where life ends and the environment begins. In geochemistry, biogenic matter is made by life but is not in itself alive; this
includes things such as coal, pearls, excrement, limestone, honey, milk,
and spider webs. This term, "biogenic matter," alerts us to the difficulty
of defining life. This "inanimate" book, for example, is northern conifer
plant detritus, from a northern conifer forest. At the same time, it is an
industrial product, a "human" artifact. Although superficially we see it
as a mere mass of paper and ink, a deeper view reveals the book to have
links beyond the human sphere to global life. Like the redwood tree, with
all its dead wood, this book is technically and literally "dead." As object,
the book is part of life's outside. Yet eventually these pages will decompose
and be churned by microorganisms or burned by fire. This book, too,
will have returned to—if it isn't already part of—the life of Earth.

On Earth, what is alive and what is not? How is life altered to become
nonlife, and vice versa? To examine this quandary, let us follow the course
of an atom of carbon on an imaginary trip through the biosphere. Coming
into my body, from a sandwich I ate, the carbon atom may already have
been spewn forth with smoke and gas from the terrestrial interior through
the mouths of volcanos some thirty times. Belched into the atmosphere
millions of years before I was born, it combined with two oxygen atoms
to become carbon dioxide, blowing about in the high winds of the tropo-
sphere for thousands of years before settling down into the ground to be
sucked up by some orange-capped mushroom, say. Eventually the fungus
died and our atom was eaten by an insect ruminating about the timber
at the forest floor. Rains came and the carbon atom moved into a stream
and then a river, wending its way into the ocean. Sinking along with the
chalky shell of a photosynthetic microbe into the oceanic abyss, the atom
stuck to the side of a submerged boulder. There it became limestone,
joining the microscopic skeletal carbon that formed part of some white
chalk cliffs. Even then the atom was not completely cut off from the
biosphere's circulation. One day, the tectonic plates moved, slamming

into each other as magma percolated inside and beneath them, shifting masses of Earth until the atom became exposed to erosion again as part of the land. The same carbon atom burped up through a volcano and into the sky and was sucked down by an avocado tree I eventually consumed as part of my whole wheat avocado-and-cheese sandwich. As part of a carbohydrate molecule, the carbon atom gave me the energy I needed to finish this sentence.

Life reigns with a Sphinxlike wholeness that is never exhausted but simply takes further sustenance from all efforts at analysis; categorizing and examining this fullness succeeds finally only in perpetuating life's mystery. The ancient Greek philosopher Heraclitus, known for his view that "being is ever becoming," compared the force that moves the world to a willful child who builds castles of stone and sand only to destroy them and start again. Heraclitus said that a person can never step in the same river twice, suggesting that the river *as a thing* must be the water that moves through it, and this water soon goes out to sea. The real river, then, must be not a thing so much as a process, one that maintains an identity despite an astounding turnover of matter. Indeed, a river is not only the water but the water's *flow*.

Even the English word "being," perhaps the most static abstract conception of which we are capable, is not static. Being is not only a "thing" but also something that happens.

All of us share this flowing, wavelike nature. Each cell in your body maintains its identity even though it incorporates over a billion different constituent molecules during its short life span. By extrapolating from tracking the turnover of radioactive atoms, it has been calculated that seven years from now virtually every atom in your body will be different. And since the calcium phosphate of your bones is dead, the bones turn over more slowly; they are less actively metabolized.

The whole blue-and-white-flecked Earth maintains itself by turning over its components. Ocean carbonate particles, limestone rocks, and animal bodies are continually moving into the soil, with the result that in less than a decade all the carbon dioxide in our atmosphere will have been replaced. In fifteen years the forests in the world will still contain many of the same trees, but each tree will contain many new atoms.

It takes 5 to 6 million years for the mass of the world's oceanic reservoir to decompose through the photosynthesizing activities of plants, algae, and cyanobacteria; hydrogen enters the dynamic bodies of these sunloving organisms while their oxygen is released into the water and air. The hydrogen and oxygen of water become the organic compounds of living things and the carbon dioxide of the Earth's atmosphere. Addressing the ocean's primal blue substance, Antoine de Saint-Exupéry wrote: "Water, you have neither taste, nor color or odor; they delight in you without knowing what you are. One cannot say that you are necessary for life; you are life itself."[2] Although Saint-Exupéry chose water as the object of his lyricism, he could have chosen mud, air, or clay. What we begin to see is that, on a global scale, the elements partaking of life exist not only within but outside of bodies as we have traditionally considered them.

The more things change, the more they stay the same.

CHAPTER 3

~

The Flowing Whole

Is There Life on Mars?

I was in California at NASA's Jet Propulsion Laboratory in 1976 when photographs from the Mars Viking I Lander were electronically relayed to Earth. Everybody was stunned by the starkness, the spectacular lack of life. Yet, it occurs to me now that there was a very striking biological form residing on the surface of the planet that went completely unnoticed precisely because it was so visible: the Lander itself! Whether you consider it a bastard offspring of the human species or a remote extension of our own flesh and blood, there can be no doubt that a robotic spacecraft—a part of life on Earth—has graced, or marred, the surface of Mars.

For years people have wondered about life on Mars. Boston astronomer Percival Lowell, whose body lies in the base of the Arizona telescope, "discovered" irrigating "canals" on the planet. On Halloween, Orson Welles made a convincing radio broadcast simulating an invasion of New York City by Martians, and many people, ignoring the disclaimers, were frightened out of their wits. When the Viking Lander plunked down, however, it found no flowing waters or agricultural fields but only a dry, ruddy desert for as far as the camera eye could see. The irony, of course, is that the camera eye itself represents the arrival of the life for which we are searching. In my mind's eye I picture lovers lolling by the

moist bed of Martian canals, a Mars covered with a latticework of waterways irrigating lemon trees and orange groves—a colorful paradise not
found but created. The Viking Lander is not incidental but integral to
this process, a tentacle of the Earth feeling out its environment through
the agency of one of its most ambitious representatives, humankind.
Whereas Lovelock believes that life must inevitably employ the atmosphere of the planet on which it dwells, and therefore cannot exist on
Mars, other scientists retain the hope that Mars may be inhabited in
remote regions or that it was once inhabited and fossil life will still be
found. The settlement of Mars is not a pipe dream but theoretically
possible right now via the new applied science of biospherics. Biospherics
has been called the second great unifying space age discipline after space
flight, or astronautics.

The disaster of the Space Shuttle Challenger underlined the fact that
astronautics is a very technical field in which human errors may be devastating. But the notion that biospherics depends in any way on human
stewardship or tending is highly misleading. The Earth has evolved
through the major Hadean, Archean, Proterozoic, and Phanerozoic
Eons—each spanning roughly a billion years and marked by radical
changes in chemical, geological, and biological conditions at the surface
of the Earth—in the total absence of human beings. According to evolutionary biologists and geologists, the Hadean Eon (4500–3900 million
years ago) was the earliest, prelife period during which the Earth's molten
surface solidified into rock. The Archean Eon (3900–2500 million years
ago), which followed, marks the beginning of life and the long tenure of
microbial life in the complete absence of plants and animals. Then came
the Proterozoic Eon (2500–580 million years ago). The early Proterozoic
Eon saw the appearance of tiny but complex nonbacterial cells that would
evolve into all plant and animal life. During this eon our modern atmosphere appeared; for the first time, gaseous oxygen accumulated in the
Earth's atmosphere. Eventually organisms too small to be seen with the
naked eye, microbes, evolved that could use what was at first, believe it
or not, a toxic gas—oxygen, which to this day still poisons many kinds
of microorganisms. Next came the Phanerozoic Eon in which we now
dwell. Even this most recent eon is 580 million years old; most of its
existence came prior to the evolution of humanity roughly 3 million years
ago (according to some). Each eon represents a biogeochemical regime
of the Earth's biosphere. Moreover, if we believe in Lovelock's Gaia

hypothesis, then each eon represents a stage in the growth of a superorganism. It is common to think that the Earth is a clump of rock whose surface is inhabited by life. But in many ways Earth does not "support a biosphere" but rather *is* one, especially for several miles at the planetary surface. Saying the Earth supports a biosphere is like saying your skeleton supports your body.

The biosphere is only in its first fledgling stages of growth into the extraterrestrial environment. Skylab, the Apollo moon shots, Soviet Venera landings on Venus, and other jaunts into orbit are like droplets splashed on bone-dry terrain. In these brief scouting expeditions, people sampled and camped out in space. No one has lived there. (Similarly, although some half million people are flying in airplanes at any given moment, no one has lived his whole life in one.) On these missions astronauts and cosmonauts bring with them what they need; they cannot stay much longer than a few weeks. Barring deep freeze-drying of living beings—so-called "lyophilization" (a technology not yet developed for large plants or mammals and one that in any case would knock out a space traveler more thoroughly than general anesthesia)—the only sensible way to set up house in space or to journey long distances is by ecological life support—biospherics.

By recycling air, water, food, and waste a person could live an entire life inside a space station or ship. Many efforts to set up permanently recycling systems are underway: aquaria, terraria, and human-sized closed-off "buildings" that provide constant supplies for those who dwell inside them. On my desk is an expensive paperweight called an "ecosphere." Supported on a plastic tripod, the glass ball is some five inches in diameter and contains seawater, bacteria, and algae. The eye follows the ecosphere's six tiny pinkish shrimp as they dart in and out of an underwater canopy of algae-covered sticks; occasionally one swims up to the surface of his puddle-sized ocean. The whole glass ball of an ecosystem, sold as an educational model by Ecospheres Associates, a research firm in Arizona, continually recycles its own wastes. Sealed by a glass nipple at the top, the ecosphere requires no watering or maintenance whatsoever, and the shrimp have lived inside it for several years. A spokesman from the company said some customers have tiny worlds containing more shrimp now than the five or six they had when the glass worlds arrived.

The frugal economy of gas and nutrient exchange exemplifies the art of mutual survival. In the privacy of these glass spheres, shrimp waste fertilizes algae. The algae convert sunlight into sugars and oxygen bubbles that provide fresh food and air for the shrimp. Meanwhile, bacteria meticulously scrape up and convert the leftovers back into raw nutrients for the other inhabitants. Compared to our big world threatened by toxic wastes, the ecological togetherness of these tiny worlds is admirable. Designed by Joseph Hanson[1] of NASA's Jet Propulsion Laboratory in California, ecospheres were developed during research on self-contained ecosystems for long-duration, manned space flight. Like the giant terraquarium of Earth, ecospheres need no cleaning, changing of water, or finagling with filters. Once created, they are self-sufficient. As long as they are in subdued sunlight at temperatures between 40 and 85° F, the shrimp remain busy, swimming with their tiny feet, munching tufts of algae, coasting past vegetation, or eyeing observers beyond their glass-encased world—a miniature biosphere you can carry in the palm of the hand. Holding one of these fragile precipitates of the Earth up to the light reminds me of Dutch artist M. C. Escher's self-portrait as reflected in and through a crystal ball. For the ecospheric crystal ball is not just an ecosphere: it is symbolic of the merging of biology, ecology, and chemistry into biospherics. It is a nip of the biogeochemical all.

From these little ecospheres on their plastic tripods we can deduce a triumph in the making. One may be tempted to dismiss them as glorified yuppie paperweights, another nature-oriented fad catering to new-age sensibilities. But ecospheres announce an astonishing fact. They speak to us of a strange pagan baptism, the rebirth of no person but of a planet. While ecospheres are closed to chemical and biological exchange but are open to particles in the form of light, the makers of ecospheres are also inventing tiny ecosystems open to chemical (but not biological) exchange with the environment. These systems permit not only light but chemical transfer: molecules that are not parts of cells can enter and exit through the walls of the experimental worlds. The containing wall of the chemically open system is so finely porous that anything larger than one-tenth of a micron is blocked from coming through; not even viruses can penetrate the chemically open systems.

Ecospheres Associates also study terrestrial (as opposed to aquatic) closed ecosystems: glass orbs containing tiny "forests" of land creatures rather than shrimp and marine organisms. Indeed, Hanson has tinkered

with over 150 "recipes" of living ingredients and is working to devise an
ecosphere of complementary organisms that include small snails and vertebrate fish. Fish are even closer to us evolutionarily than are shrimp.
Hanson's experimental designs represent a level of ecological play that
not only goes beyond mere technological tinkering but is, in fact, more
than human. I've said previously that the biosphere is preparing to reproduce. From a biospheric vantage point, the human creation of these
tiny self-sufficient ecosystems is a form of *necessary play*—reminiscent of
childhood games such as dressing up and playing house with friends and
dolls. In the biospheric merging of agriculture and architecture we lay
our collective head in the lap of nature and dream of a cosmic future
that may in a sense already have been.

It's too bad Escher is not alive today to sketch one of these things.
What fun he might have. For the strange symmetry of the ecosphere
displays not only an image of a global living space but also foreshadows
or reflects human futures, ecological collectives in which life forms in-
termesh and nonlinearly self-organize to become more than their simple
sum. Looking into the crystal ball on my desk I see a version of where
and how humans will live in coming millennia. As Eugene A. Cernan,
the last man to walk on the moon (in December 1972), put it, "You can't
return home without feeling that difference. But you do come back to
reality very quickly. You try to share and relate your feelings to others,
but you can't take a billion people back with you. It's almost as if you
have come back from the future."[2] The shift is that with biospherics, the
technology broached by these ecospheres, a billion people can share directly in the experience of space flight. With biospherics humankind gains
the potential not only to visit the moon, Mars, and beyond, but to live
there permanently, in ecological self-sufficiency beyond the umbilical
cord of Mother Earth. The ecospheres are microcosms not only of the
biosphere but of the future.

While some ecospheres have already supported shrimp in isolation for
over five years, tiny, closed ecosystems containing nonanimal life have
been even more successful. Communities of bacteria have been living
and dying, generation after generation, in sunlit sealed laboratory flasks
since 1967 (as good a time to be conceived as any). The new improved
petri dishes were designed by Clair Folsome, late professor of microbiology

at the University of Hawaii. Folsome, a leading expert on closed-systems ecology, along with colleague Elizabeth Kearns, maintained their living microbial captives for the intervening years with no perceptible loss in photosynthetic productivity. Measurements of carbon flux rates and oxygen partial pressures have demonstrated that biological productivity has not decreased over the nearly two-decade period of closure. The natives remain healthy and restless; they regularly change colors from green to purple-red as the populations inside grow and recede.

Folsome believed such communities can in principle stay alive forever. So here we have, in a tiny vial, a tantalizing hint of cosmic immortality. Are Folsome's innocent-seeming glass-enclosed laboratory communities really among the Earth's first human-engineered "seeds"? Are we seeing here early signs of a movement ultimately destined to fructify, to bring to life the entire cosmos? Assuming it is not already alive?

Whenever animals indulge in sexual activity they physiologically revert to the hot swampy time of life's origins, to their microbial ancestry; they produce fluids and eject haploid germ cells in the ancient gamble of regeneration. Bearing in mind the microbial connection to sex, and sex's connection to the immortality of new generations, where might we find the inhabitants and descendants of Folsome's tiny arks in future eons? In, say, 5 million years? Or rather, where might we *not* find them? Which is to say that in 5 million years life may be virtually everywhere.

But that is not all. Replenishing land capsules made and inhabited by the Soviets have kept people alive and provided with food throughout the long Siberian winter. The builders of "Biosphere II" hope to provide an infrastructure to contain several "biospherians" for two or more years. Such fascinating engineering projects suggest that someday people may be in the position of the shrimp inside an ecosphere, the captives and crews of biospheric starships sheltered in spacecraft that double as synthetic Earths. As Buckminster Fuller noted, we are *already* on a space-faring craft whirling through space and containing its own biosphere: the so-called Spaceship Earth. In this worldly sense, the science-fiction future we are waiting for has indeed already arrived.

Vernadsky's Biosphere

Though he did not coin the term, Russian scientist Vladimir Vernadsky was the first to give currency to the word "biosphere." "The biosphere," Vernadsky wrote, "is the environment in which we live, it is the 'nature' that surrounds us and to which we refer in common parlance."[3] Austrian geologist Edward Suess first used the term in 1875 in a slim book on how mountains arise. Suess pointed out that "One thing seems to be foreign on this large celestial body consisting of spheres, namely— organic life. . . . On the surface of continents it is possible to single out a self-contained biosphere."[4]

Vernadsky first encountered the term in reading Suess's last work, a multivolume treatise called *The Face of the Earth*, a monumental synthesis of all geology up to that time, composed between 1883 and 1909. Despite this introduction of the word into the scientific literature, it did not catch on at first except among a few intellectuals studying in Paris after World War I.

Among those who enthusiastically embraced the term biosphere, and explored the implications of its use from the start, were Vernadsky and his contemporaries Edouard Le Roy (philosopher Henri Bergson's successor at the College de France) and Pierre Teilhard de Chardin, the well-known "evolutionary theologian" who was then professor of geology at the *Institut Catholique* in Paris. The biosphere concept, elaborated by both Vernadsky and Chardin, implies that life is not simply a matter of individual plants and animals but is a planetary phenomenon. The related term "noosphere"—referring to the sphere of human influence on the planet—also used by both men, but in very different ways, is first bandied about in Le Roy's books but may have arisen during a meeting of Chardin, Le Roy, and Vernadsky in Paris during the 1920s. Whereas noosphere for Chardin was the "human" planetary layer forming "outside and above the biosphere," for Vernadsky the noosphere referred to humanity and technology but as inside and part of the planetary biosphere. Swiss historian Jacques Grinevald explains that the distinct purposes to which the theistic Chardin and the atheistic Vernadsky put these terms have lead to the duality of the term biosphere as currently used: on the one hand, biosphere refers to the zone in which life exists (which was the way Vernadsky usually employed it); on the other hand, it means the totality of life itself (as Chardin used it).

To see the different connotations of these two usages of the word biosphere, picture that instructive old redwood tree. Even though only the outer part may be growing, we think of the entire tree—including its "dead" wood and bark—as being alive. The biosphere also is alive in this Vernadskian sense of the term that refers not only to actively growing life but to the zone or envelope in which life exists in a more mute or structural state. Generally speaking, Vernadsky's usage refers to the whole tree, Chardin's only to the most active regions of growth. The Earth as living being may be seen in a similar way. We may refer to it as alive in the narrow "Chardinian" sense; or we may see the chalky cliffs, the organic-rich oceans, and the clouds not as inert environment but as part of the extensive body of a unified thing that is living and growing as a whole. Where precisely this entity ends is, of course, open to question.

Vladimir Ivanovich Vernadsky was born in St. Petersburg on March 12, 1863. His father was a political economist and statistician, and Vernadsky wrote that an intellectual awakening of sorts took place during his youth on walks with his father and his father's cousin, retired military officer Yevgraf Maksimovich Korolenko. Under the starlit skies, the grey-bearded Korolenko would philosophize. An atheist familiar with the works of French naturalists Jean Baptiste Pierre Antoine de Monet de Lamarck and Comte de Georges Louis Leclere Buffon, as well as British geologist Sir Charles Lyell and naturalist Charles Darwin, "Uncle" Korolenko speculated that life existed upon other planets, that thought and matter were inseparable and each could give rise to the other, that matter was transferred on a worldwide scale by plants and animals, and that the Earth was a living organism. Six years after his mentor Korolenko died, Vernadsky wrote "It sometimes seems to me that I must work not only for myself, but for him as well, and that not only my life but his life as well, will have been lived in vain if I accomplish nothing."[5] His early exposure to Korolenko's ideas provided Vernadsky with lifelong inspiration. Vernadsky broadened his studies. He became interested in the effects of solar radiation on life, and of life upon itself and the surface of the Earth. All the while he maintained that "The right of freedom of thought for me is one of the most necessary preconditions for a normal life, and I could never tolerate the lack of it."[6]

Originally a mineralogist and crystallographer, Vernadsky came to biology through his realization that the properties of soil could not be understood without taking into account the enormous influence of the living beings that help form soil and which soil contains. Vernadsky came to use the word biosphere to mean more than a thin film at the Earth's surface. The study of soil provided a focus for the interaction of life and minerals, for a view in which life was a special kind of mineral, part of a planetary chemical reaction. Vernadsky came to believe that the diversity of life forms, far from being incidental to the planet's surface, were essential to many of the minerals of the Earth's crust. The thin layer of living matter made an impact out of all proportion to the scanty space it occupied. He believed that, of all the geological forces acting on the surface of the Earth, living matter was the greatest and its force increased with time. We can see Vernadsky's "force of life" in the horizontal spreading of life to all parts of the Earth's surface, as well as in its ascent from the oceanic depths to the land and atmosphere beyond.

Vernadsky retained the childlike wonder of his walks with Korolenko. Sparked by this youthful insight and keen perception, he continued to be amazed with the ways of nature, even after others felt such ways were well understood and had been adequately explained.

Vernadsky looked at life—properly the subject matter of biology— from a standpoint beyond biology. He merged the chemist's microanalysis of molecular formation with the cosmic perspective of the astronomer. To him living matter was an organic mineral with some very unusual properties. It was a mineral whose energy and ever more creative activities derived from the sun. For Vernadsky the Earth was in material communion with the sun: the Earth was not just the Earth but part of the Earth-solar system. He wrote:

> The biosphere is as much, or even more, the creation of the Sun as it is a manifestation of earthly processes. Ancient religious intuitions which regarded terrestrial creatures, especially human beings as "children of the Sun" were much nearer the truth than those which looked upon them as a mere ephemeral creation, a blind and accidental product of matter and earth-forces. Terrestrial creatures are the fruit of a long and complicated cosmic process and, subject to predetermined laws, form a necessary part of a harmonious cosmic mechanism in which chance does not exist.[7]

Vernadsky pictured life on Earth as a global chemical reaction, a "green burning."[8] Where others saw groups of species and organisms, Vernadsky saw patches and films of atoms collecting and migrating under the influence of the sun. A radiation-trapping and -transforming mineral, life spreads and grows, it coalesces and disseminates, it merges and diverges with itself. In his ultramaterialistic perspective, Vernadsky saw through the word "life" to a strange solar-powered mineral. The alimentary pathways of the Earth form from minerals, from living beings, and the matter they eke and leak out then environmentalizes and assimilates into their own physical natures in an unending game of material transformation. Life is not life but rock rearranging itself under the sun.

After lifelong study, Vernadsky reached two major conclusions that he calls biogeochemical principles. The first is that "The biogenic migration of the atoms of chemical elements in the biosphere always tends to its maximum manifestation." In other words, atoms that form and reform organisms become busier as life forms expand under optimal conditions. The second is that "The evolution of species in the course of geological time, leading to the creation of life forms that are stable in the biosphere, proceeds in a direction which increases the biogenic migration of atoms in the biosphere."[9] Here Vernadsky seems to have in mind such things as enzymes—proteins with the special property of dramatically increasing the rates of chemical reactions that, outside organisms, take place very slowly. Vernadsky's second principle can also be seen to apply to biospheres, in which the recycling of elements crucial to life must of necessity proceed at a much more rapid pace than occurs in the original biosphere of the outside world. Vernadsky's second principle suggests that the biosphere favors organisms that rapidly mix chemical elements about the planetary surface, either by their doings or merely in the reproducing necessary to sustain themselves as beings.

For Vernadsky, as for Heraclitus, whirl and change and flux is the main, if paradoxical, constant of life on earth. We may look at organisms and species, but we may also look at the more elementary movements of atoms in flux. Our atmosphere, for example, contains rapidly moving, chemically anomalous particulates of calcium, carbon, and phosphorus: we call them sea gulls. So, too, 100 trillion ants in the Amazon add about 55,000 tons of formic acid a year to the environment, generating maybe one-fourth of all the acid rain there. Fungi on rotting trees leak some 5 million tons of chlorocarbons into the atmosphere a year by disseminating their spores. These examples suggest a way of looking at life that reduces familiar organisms down to their chemical essentials, not in order to belittle them but as a way to see the Earth's giant metabolic system.

Lovelock's Gaia hypothesis states that the temperature and chemical composition of the Earth's atmosphere, sediments, and oceans are regulated by organisms in the manner of a living body or cybernetic system. Although Vernadsky never regarded the Earth as a giant being, endowed with its own physiology, his work helps to dismantle the fence that has been erected between biology and geology. If animals and algae are really weird forms of rock, we must be far more a part of the environment than we thought.

In a sense, Vernadsky did for biological space what Darwin did for biological time: he showed that the main traits, the scientific character of life as a whole, could be best grasped on a global scale, one that encompasses space and radiations from the sun. As Darwin led life to contemplate its ancient past by showing how all live beings descend from the same ancestors, Vernadsky extended the province of inquiry from local investigation to life on a planetary scale. And Vernadsky, like Darwin, did not balk when applying his way of seeing to humankind. He did not exempt us from his mineralogical analysis of life: indeed, we epitomize Vernadsky's principle that over evolutionary time more and more chemicals become involved with life and circulate throughout the biosphere, that the rate of this circulation becomes faster and faster. The overall effect of biological change was and is to increase the pace and scope of atomic movement. New species have new abilities; they evolve different modes of nutrition and move to unexploited niches. In so doing, they extend to new lengths the already rapid biospheric circulation. Our technical civilization brings into circulation and combines many substances—such as pharmaceutical compounds, metals (for example, the platinum of weapons and the copper of pennies), rubberlike plastics, and other synthetics that were rarely or never used by other organisms. Garbage disposals, jet airplanes, and factory exhaust increase the rate of atomic migration at the Earth's surface. Since Vernadsky's death, physicists have even synthesized elements that never before existed at the surface of the Earth. With worldwide commerce and computer communication, the flow of atoms intensifies. With the appearance of *Homo sapiens, all* the chemical elements for the first time became involved in the process of life, the biologically aided circulation of elements at our planet's surface.

Though Vernadsky was not revered in his time (indeed, his papers were for many years shelved and ignored), Russian writings now refer to him as "the father of the teachings of the biosphere" and the most important geochemical institute in the Soviet Union bears his name. In many ways it is remarkable that Vernadsky, who died in 1945 before the end of World War II, could form a truly global vision—in which life continually changes the geology and chemistry of the Earth's surface—before the dawn of the space age. With the October 1957 orbiting of Sputnik, the Soviets launched the space race. Later, on April 21, 1961, the 27-year-old Soviet air force pilot Yuri Gargarin flew with Vostoc I into orbit, thereby inaugurating the space age as well as becoming the first human to gaze at Earth as a place—a kind of vast, spherical fishtank—he had left. In remembering Vernadsky, we should recall that he came up with a gestalt view of the biosphere as a solar, terraqueous being, and that he did so before modern astronautics, the Apollo moon shot, or the space photographs that are now common currency. In his 1930 book *Geochimie*, Vernadsky wrote, "We are living in a critical epoch of the history of mankind"; what is emerging, he wrote, is "the idea and feeling of the Whole."[10]

What Is Life?

Surely, by discussing the biosphere as a biological system or organism the size of a planet we broaden our definition of life. And defining life is definitely a problem; many biology textbooks to this day give no or inadequate definitions of life. It is fairly easy to deconstruct—to take apart—and show the inadequacy of any definition of life.

The *Encyclopaedia Britannica*, for example, lists five definitions for life under its entry.[11]

The first is physiological: a definition of life in which entities capable of physiological functions such as eating, excreting, metabolizing, reproducing, and responding to external stimuli are classified as alive. But, as the article itself remarks, under this definition automobiles, which take in fuel, excrete exhaust, and are proliferated in vast numbers, might be classified as alive.

The second definition given by the *Encylopaedia* is metabolic: "an object with a definite boundary, continually exchanging some of its materials with its surroundings, but without altering its general properties, at least over some period of time." But the simple example of spores, seeds, and other forms of life that remain dormant for up to hundreds of years would mean that a walnut is not alive. In addition, as the article again points out, the well-defined shape of a flame has a fixed boundary and is maintained by burning a combination of hydrogen-rich wax and oxygen, giving off carbon dioxide and water. In a conflagration, flames even grow. So the metabolic definition is also inadequate.

A molecular biological definition is given third, in which organisms are defined as systems that "contain reproducible hereditary information coded in nucleic acid molecules and that metabolize by controlling the rate of chemical reactions using proteinaceous catalysts known as enzymes." But the problem with this definition is that it defines life in terms of the specific materials used for life on Earth. I once argued with Mexican scientist Antonio Lazcano whether machines could ever be considered alive; on the basis of my readings of Samuel Butler, machines were capable of life at some remote point in the future and, in a certain sense, they are already alive. Lazcano said, no, machines are not alive. But, I said, what if, in the remote future, silicon computers were to arise capable not only of consciousness and philosophical reflection, but of begetting their own offspring from spare metal parts? Wouldn't he concede that these must be alive? No, he insisted, life, *by definition*, must be carbon-based—as we are. The problem with the biochemical or molecular biological definition is that it dismisses out of hand any form of life that is not exactly like the life we know on Earth.

According to the fourth, thermodynamic, definition of life, living systems are "localized regions where there is a continuous increase in order." This is accomplished by a decrease in order around them. The problem with this definition is that certain chemical reactions exhibit negative entropy, an increase in order, complexity, and beauty that is, nonetheless, clearly not alive.

The preferred and fifth definition is the genetic one: "a system capable of evolution by natural selection." The problem here is that for organisms to evolve by natural selection they must reproduce. A hybrid such as a mule, however, is clearly alive although it cannot reproduce. Nonetheless, as the article states, the composite cells of even a sterile organism, in this case a mule, do reproduce. It is worth noting that, according to this definition, the biosphere *by definition* cannot be alive unless it not only reproduces but undergoes natural selection. Even if man-made biospheres are interpreted as reproductive replicas of Earth, we must wait—according to this definition—until some live and some die before pronouncing life a planetary phenomenon. While perhaps the strongest of the five definitions, the genetic definition of life fails because it is possible to imagine an organism that lives without ever reproducing: indeed, the first cell to have evolved, before it reproduced, may have been in a position similar to that of a reproductively immature Gaia—an organism arising abiotically, not from a parent but from nonlife. Can we give the concept of life a firmer ground, one independent of the notion of reproduction? Scientifically, the origin of life from nonlife is of great interest, and scientists have succeeded in forming many lifelike compounds. But philosophically the origin of life from nonlife may be a sort of materialistic conundrum. We have not yet defined life. We have not found its essence, its outer limit. What is it?

Alan Watts wrote that "we tend to think of this planet as life-infested rock, which is as absurd as thinking of the body as a cell-infested skeleton."[12] A translator of ancient Buddhist texts into idiomatic English, Watts suggests there is no escape from the conclusion that the whole universe is, in a certain sense, alive. But if everything is alive, what is life? On this question, Watts quotes German Nobel prize–winning quantum physicist Erwin Schrödinger, whose "What is Life?"—written before the discovery of DNA—inspired a whole generation of biologists.

> Thus you can throw yourself flat on the ground, stretched out upon mother Earth, with the certain conviction that you are one with her and she with you. You are as firmly established, as invulnerable as she, indeed a thousand times firmer and more invulnerable. As surely as she will engulf you tomorrow, so surely will she bring you forth anew to new striving and suffering. And not merely "some day": now, today, every day she is bringing you forth, not *once* but thousands upon thousands of times, just as every day she engulfs you a thousand times over. For eternally and always there is only *now*; the present is the only thing that has no end.[13]

A remarkable passage, to be sure. And these somewhat mystical views are, I must confess, close to my own. But even with the discovery of DNA and numerous cellular and molecular biological mechanisms, Schrödinger's timeless question remains, "What is Life?"

Lovelock has suggested that our difficulty in defining life may be due to its status as an ancient survival mechanism. (Lovelock told me his own charmingly literary definition that life is something "edible, lovable, or lethal." This is incorrect, of course, since many things—like lightning—are lethal but are not considered alive.) But Lovelock means that from an evolutionary viewpoint recognizing what eats, makes love or kills was necessary for our survival long before the origin of language. We retain cognition of life at a preverbal level, as in the primeval fear induced in some by the sight of a spider or a snake, animals presumably more difficult to define than to kill or to flee. Smell and sickness warn of noxious microbes; on the other hand, walking in the fragrant woods or listening to singing birds can be a definite mood enhancer. Such responses are definite but undefined, for it is as difficult to mark an outline on life as it is to reach into the beach and capture a wave. We may recognize the wave and be borne aloft by its power; we may know it when we see it and dive into it with joy. But we cannot take it home in a bottle or a test tube, put it on a shelf, and make of it some final and definitive characterization. That is because, even at home or in the laboratory, we are not outside the wave.

Definition means limitation, marking boundaries with an outline. The opposite of a definition I take to be a pun, such as the following visual one: we must develop a feeling for the (w)hole. Puns and their kin, homonyms, portmanteau words, rhymes, and so forth, cannot be pinned down. They are like the space suggested and the outline left open in a charcoal drawing; they do not delineate, circumscribe, and section off like a definition, but, rather, leave us in a state of undecidedness and ambiguity, a state that the reader or viewer must work with his or her own mind to complete. With the gracefulness of butterflies, puns elude the efforts of the metaphysical materialist to capture and mount them in some museum case of fixed meaning, and this polysemy of theirs is as much a liability as it is a blessing. For me, for example, the "w" of the "whole" belongs to the wave. The wave is ultimately neither process nor metaphor, for process and metaphor are both only words, signs, and labels we can dismiss. But the wave "waves." It spills and flows over itself to become what it is not. Like Narcissus crouching over a still pond, we may look at a photograph of the watery Earth and recognize for the first time our own body. A perceptual shift occurs in which the definition of life changes as the boundaries of our environmental concern broadens. The definition breaks open.

The humorous definition of life as "animated water," was one Vernadsky repeated and admired. Vernadsky catalogued water into a variety of types, considering it a mineral with many forms, or even many different minerals. But life as mineral also has its solid phase, its numb body, the hard house it carries with it or which carries it. Thus, for geochemistry a swarm of locusts flying over the Red Sea—which one tends to think of as a sky-darkening invasion or an agricultural scourge—is an airborne stream of rock. "What is a swarm of locusts from the biogeochemical point of view?" Vernadsky asks in his *Works*. It "is, as it were, a disperse of rock, extremely active chemically, and found in motion."[14] As geologist Lapo points out:

> [No researcher before Vernadsky approached] living matter from such a standpoint. Living organisms were under the jurisdiction of the "biological department," and it occurred to nobody that living matter could be regarded as rock. The reason, evidently, was that this rock was of a specific kind. . . . Living matter of the biosphere is characterized by tremendous free energy. In the inorganic world only unsolidified lava streams are comparable to living matter in the quantity of free energy. They are, perhaps, even richer in energy, but quite short-lived.[15]

Geochemically, a swarm of locusts is the point of transformation of one section of the biosphere into another. It is a flying mountain. In 1890, G. T. Carruthers calculated that the weight of a swarm of locusts, documented to have covered the sky above the Red Sea for two days and a night, was 44 million tons. The plague of locusts descended on fertile Mesopotamian fields, devoured everything, and then flew to Ethiopia. This quantity of transported mass equals all the zinc and copper mined throughout the nineteenth century.[16]

When life is subsumed under the category of geology, continental drift, radical as it once was, becomes less so. For not only the tectonic movements of continents but the thousands of passengers traveling in the air at any moment, the continental swarms of automobiles, the orbiting, spinning satellites—all life and technology—also come under the heading of geology. We are bits of matter that have come detached from the Earth and are moving around. And if we believe Vernadsky's second biogeochemical principle, the rate of this movement is increasing dramatically as we move forward in evolutionary time.

The medieval notion of a live universe and the geochemical concept of living matter as a kind of mineral are akin. Both suggest in their ways that the planet is a system. Living matter is not only a fluctuation of minerals but a physiological whole. If we agree that we inhabit a living Earth, and that the biosphere is, in many ways, undergoing stress or sickness as the result of human technological success, then the next steps are to diagnose and to treat that illness. This cannot even begin to be done until we grasp the external environment as an active, sensing, and responsive body.

Swiss-born alchemist and physician Philippus Aureolus Paracelsus (Theophrastus Bombastus von Hohenheim) counseled his sixteenth-century contemporaries to study their "external anatomy." Such a view, taken seriously, alters our perception and treatment of the environment. However arduously, our body and home grow. Realizing that the outside is inside is a major, vertiginous shift. We begin to become attentive to the Earth as we might listen to and care for our own ailing or healthy body. The attentiveness of Paracelsus to the environment helped him discover that metals lay beneath plants that looked sick and yellow or grey in color. Studying external anatomy was also pragmatic; Paracelsus was probably the first person to apply biogeochemistry to the prospecting of resources. Today, biogeochemical methods are used by major corporations to find deposits of coal and oil.

So we have two views: the view that the world is alive, and the notion that we are minerals. Both share the virtue of focusing attention upon the interrelation of human beings with the environment. In addition, the Gaian view of a living Earth is far more sophisticated, from a scientific standpoint, than any fuzzy medieval notions of the individual as a microcosm, a miniature copy of the living universe. Its true discourse, as we shall see, is not that of the occult, or even of philosophy, but of science itself. If I have discussed philosophical concepts first, and scientific ones second, it is because I believe that science is rooted in philosophy, not the other way around.

What would it mean to rethink life from zero? If we cannot say *what* life is, perhaps we can at least say *where* it is. According to the language of my friend David Abram, a magician with an interest in perception and ecology as well as a philosopher, life does not live *on* the Earth but *in* the Earth. Life dwells in water: in the sediments, oceans, rivers, lakes, swamps, marshes, deserts, bogs, snow, and air. Abram has used his sleight-of-hand skills to make inroads in anthropology. Performing for people from cultures ranging from the Nepalese to the Bedouin Arabs of the Sinai desert, he has found that, without being particularly gullible, many people still view nature as alive.

Some cultures may still see nature the way we experience a magic show. Our Western way of seeing emphasizes objectivity, separates body and mind, and ethnocentrically assures us that it is right. But it may be that the mythic view of nature as magical and alive is closer to the mark.

In traditional cultures the shaman serves as a go-between between the human and nonhuman living realms. Abram recounts the story of a "medicine man," an old shaman in Santa Fe, New Mexico, who pointed to a stone and told him it too was alive. "If I can see this stone," said the medicine man, "it must be alive." Insofar as it affects tides and draws up waves that distribute nutrients, insofar as it cyclically influences life on Earth, the moon too is part of life, of life rethought. The whole universe is interrelated. Contemporary physics has demolished the neat separation between the observer and the observed. Though at the distant horizon of our daily experience, even the rock-solid moon is part of us.

CHAPTER 4

~

Metapatterns

In *Mind and Nature: A Necessary Unit*, Gregory Bateson, searching for a "pattern which connects all living creatures," explores the similarities between ecological and psychological processes, showing that recursive or cybernetic processes exist in both.[1] Perhaps this pattern (or "metapattern," as Bateson calls it) has been found. Life changes to stay the same. Chilean biologists Humberto Maturana and Francisco Varela have named this changing to stay the same "autopoiesis."[2] Autopoiesis entails the turning over of matter, and the turnover of matter applies at many levels. The single cell is the simplest level of what acts alive. From even simpler components, a unicell makes itself, synthesizing proteins, lipids, enzymes, and other complex carbon chemicals. A cell is a complex living unit, consisting on the average of some 10,000 different proteins. Yet in its lifetime this entire macromolecular population of a cell—whether it is swimming beneath the glass coverslip of a laboratory slide or coursing through my bloodstream—will completely interchange with its surroundings some 10,000 times. Systems theorist Milan Zeleny writes:

> Throughout this staggering turnover of matter the cell maintains its distinctiveness, cohesiveness, and relative autonomy. It produces myriads of components, yet it does not produce only something else—*it produces itself*. A cell maintains its identity and distinctiveness even

49

though it incorporates at least 10^9 [1 billion] different constitutive molecules during its life span. This maintenance of unity and wholeness, while the components themselves are being continuously or periodically disassembled and rebuilt, created and decimated, produced and consumed, is called "autopoiesis."[3]

But does autopoiesis also apply to groups of organisms and to planetary life as a whole? Autopoiesis might be a candidate for Bateson's metapattern connecting all living creatures. It is, as its Chilean describers point out, a *sine qua non* of life; and as the title of their book, *Autopoiesis and Cognition*, suggests, autopoiesis, producing oneself, describes not only the physiological realm of cells but also the more subtle realm of mental processes. For Maturana and Varela, the strange closure at work in autopoiesis also marks cognition, linking nature inseparably to mind.

Although at first glance it is a far cry from the academic discipline of biology, art may epitomize the "poietic" process at work in life. Listen to painter Willem de Kooning describe the act of writing:

If you write down a sentence and you don't like it, but that's what you wanted to say, you say it again in another way. Once you start doing it and you find how difficult it is, you get interested. You have it, then you lose it again, and then you get it again. You have to change to stay the same.[4]

"Autopoiesis" comes from the same Greek root as poetry, *poieîn*, meaning to bring forth or create. Beings arrange themselves from the substances around them no less than writers form poems from disparate words. We may even get the impression that nature writes itself and leaves its own signature covertly in the physicality of the text and in the absence and plenitude of meanings that no writer can ever completely control.

A cell is autopoietic. But so may be the biosphere, the planetary system of interweaving interconnected life forms. James Hutton, a medical doctor and a founder of modern geology, wrote that "The matter of this active world is perpetually moved, in that salutary circulation by which provision is so wisely made for the growth and prosperity of plants, and for the life and comfort of the various animals."[5]

Before the rise of the nineteenth century and the mechanical view that everything can be explained by forces acting on particles, many scientists accepted the concept of a living Earth. In a lecture to the Royal Society of Edinburgh in 1785, Hutton stated, "I consider the Earth to be a superorganism and that its proper study should be by physiology."[6] Hutton, inspired by the discovery of the circulation of the blood, noticed that similar circulation processes occur on the surface of the Earth, for example in the hydrologic cycle of flowing water—evaporation and rains.

Nonetheless, as Lovelock points out, historically two concepts of evolution arose, one for the Earth and one for life.[7] Although life and its environment are inseparable, the two were studied in separate academic departments, as if the Earth were not a single entity that evolved through time. From Victorian times onward, academia, adhering to ever more specialized disciplines, has asserted that life is one thing, under the province of biology, while Earth is another, whose proper study is geology. This separation has resulted in the view that life, separate from the environment in which it is located, *adapts* to that environment. According to Lovelock, the "apartheid of Victorian biology and geology" is beginning to crumble as theories of coevolution gain stature and the complex interaction between life and environment becomes increasingly recognized.[8]

The apartheid is only really destroyed by the Gaia hypothesis, which considers the chemical composition and climate of the Earth as a single physiological system, a live entity. Traditional academics, Lovelock notes, use the equations but have overlooked the words of theoretical ecologist Alfred Lotka, who wrote in 1925 that "It is not so much the organism or the species that evolves, but the entire system, species plus environment. The two are inseparable."[9] Mainstream academics seem not to realize the extent to which the universe differs from a university. The Earth, unlike academia, has never been departmentalized into geography, geology, agriculture, soil sciences, meteorology, and so on. Instead, the planet is, and always was, a single integrated system; the divisions are mental. It is true that chronologically the human brain evolved long after microbial life enveloped the planetary surface. And yet it also seems clear that environmental variables, such as the oxygen content of the atmosphere, have been actively regulated by microbial life for millions of years. Philosophically, Earth cannot be untied from mind.

The human drama itself depends on the Earth, a central reservoir that lends indispensable material not only to us but to all members of the millions of species inhabiting the planetary surface. The priceless wealth of the Earth can be measured in numerous ways. Estimates for the number of species range from several to more than 30 million. Life as a whole weighs in at an estimated 2½ trillion tons, dry weight. And though much of this biomass contains DNA, it is not homogenous. A single gram of soil may contain 400 million bacteria, 2 million fungal spores, and 100,000 protoctists (miscellaneous microbes such as algae, slime molds, ciliates, and so on)—not to mention animals, plants, and their parts such as earthworms, insect eggs, nematodes, rotifers, seeds, coffee grounds, and so on. Exposed to different environments—different chemical, biological, and weather conditions—the organisms in this gram of soil will differentially reproduce; they will sprout, hatch, develop, and colonize; in so doing, they will spill over into their environment, weaving in and out of it, exuding feces and laying parts of it to waste. Therefore they create new sets of conditions less suitable for them than for other organisms.

Earth itself is created by the metabolism of the living creatures it contains. The gasoline we pour into our cars is a biological product; the surface of this planet is so interwoven with life and its products that any separation of the organic from the inorganic remains ideal, abstract. Even dirt is a waiting form of life: researchers at Boston University found more than 115 different types of desiccation-resistant microorganisms present in seaside muck; the organisms, none of them plants or animals, that grew upon being wetted in the laboratory were not common in the field. We walk over mud, considering it excrescence—excess and waste. But this waste, when its constituents are rearranged, brings forth a stew—on which organisms feed, in which other organisms grow, and without which the organic recombination known as man, which from a biospheric vantage point is also a kind of excess, would remain unthinkable.

The Limits of Art

In northeast Spain, at Figueras, there is a museum devoted to Salvador Dali. Wandering through the corridor on the ground floor of this museum, one gets a feeling for some of the surrealist's love of ambiguity. One giant canvas viewed close seems to be an abstract painting of colors; looking through a specially provided scope from an angle, the painting resolves into an accurate portrait of Abraham Lincoln with beard and stovepipe hat. Still stranger are a series of "sculptures," consisting only of ordinary rocks Dali has grouped together and arranged at eye level. The rocks are arranged in a pattern to look like the bodies of reclining women: the women at the rocky beach *are* the beach.

Such works are visual puns, objects of art that recall the "natural ambiguity" of beings that are alive. We breathe, eat, walk, talk, write, and think. Yet we are made like Dali's women-rocks of objects found at the surface of the Earth. The abundance of elements in our bodies mirrors the abundance of elements in the universe at large. What Heidegger would call our "thingly nature"[10] flashes out toward consciousness. Life is a material. It is a mineral, Vernadsky's geological phenomenon. In fact, the nature of matter comes into its own, is seen most clearly, when that matter is arranged as life. Graphite is never more graphite, wood never more wood than when I bear down on this pencil to inscribe these words. The calcium phosphate of human bones is never more so than when it moves inside the fingers leafing through these pages. "I" look in the mirror and see a strange thing indeed: I see matter corresponding with its own nature. Or rather, objects—through me—recognize their own nature. I am here but there is no "me."

Marine creatures known as chitons (or sea cradles), a form of mollusk, have rows of red and black teeth to scrape algae off underwater coral. The reddish teeth are made of the inorganic iron mineral form ferrous hydrate; the black ones are of magnetite. These teeth are as metallic and as "dead" as a set of nail clippers. The radula, or scraping apparatus capped with tiny iron teeth, of chitons are harder than the chalky reefs they scrape while eating. The rocks, at least some of them, are alive.

In biologically controlled mineralization, an organism's body determines the structure of a mineral or crystal. We see this in the production of the black teeth inside the chiton's body from precursors that thicken and harden. Unlike igneous and metamorphic rocks, produced by the great pressures and high temperatures found inside the Earth, organisms can make minerals at room temperature under just one atmosphere of pressure. Chitons make not only iron but also calcium, such as crystalline dolomite, a fluorinated form of calcium phosphate, the same material that makes up our teeth and bones. And chitons do so throughout the biosphere, from arctic environments to tropical waters, from the one atmosphere of pressure found at the Earth's surface to the more than 100 atmospheres of pressure prevailing in the ocean depths.

Magnetite formed by chiton was once thought to be a unique example of biological mineral processing. But now we know such processing does not occur only with chitons. All organisms have a "thingly nature." Human teeth, for example, are converted toxic waste dumps: evolutionarily, my teeth derive from the need of marine cells to dump calcium waste outside their cell membranes. Calcium is a mineral that will wreak havoc with normal cellular metabolism. Trucking this hazardous waste across cell lines in ancestral colonies of marine cells may well be the basis of all present-day shell- and bone-making.

To this day, life acts as a "poor artist" with no money to spend on fancy materials: prevalent calcium minerals (such as calcite, aragonite, carbonate, phosphate, halite, gypsum, and so forth) are also the dominant media used in biomineralization. Opal, a semiprecious type of silica known for its iridescent play of colors, comes next. And the magnetic mineral magnetite, far from being confined to the caps of chiton teeth, has been found inside the cells of bacteria, in swimming forms of algae, and in minute quantities in the brains of migratory fish, birds, sea turtles, and honeybees. In many of these species it may act as a compass. While there are only a limited number of materials on the Earth's surface, the uses to which they can be put seem almost infinite. The segregation and distillation by life of minerals runs counter to entropy, the universal tendency toward chaos and disorder; and biomineralization is a prerequisite to geophysiology, allowing the Earth as a whole to build up systems of chemical intricacy reminiscent, if not definitive, of a living organism. The worldwide siphoning of silica by subvisible marine diatoms, and the equally massive removal of calcium carbonate by other microbes, anatomically and physiologically help change the Earth from a mere planet into a celestial *body*.

Planetary biomineralization is not only massive but subtle. Oppossum shrimp use fluorite crystals to avoid the light. These shrimp produce near-perfect, needle-shaped fluorite crystals, which is unlike the fluorite produced by magma inside the Earth. And, unlike the "poor artist" organisms that produce minerals from environmentally abundant materials, these shrimp create their crystals from environmentally scarce resources. Phosphorus, an absolutely critical compound for the manufacture of intracellular biological materials, is also scarce on the surface of the earth: with respect to phosphorus, all organisms are "fine artists."

Beautifully symmetrical marine microbes known as radiolarians deplete the oceans of amorphous silica and strontium to produce their ornate skeletons. A shrub in New Zealand has reportedly been found whose dried leaves contain up to 1 percent of nickel—a greater percentage than some mineral sources currently being mined. The concentration of vanadium in marine animals known as ascidians rivals the concentration of iron in ours; and yet vanadium is much more rare. These details from the natural world remind me of some of the transformations painted by Belgian surrealist René Magritte. Like a brown wine bottle represented to became a carrot in the painting entitled "The Explanation," or his depictions of pointy leaves broadening into the shape of green-beaked birds, life forms itself from the palette of whatever is available: flowers grow from soil; fungi grow from trees. A petrified forest intrigues us precisely because wood becomes rock. In art and nature, there is a difference between what an object is made of and what an object is. Distinct materials fill the same forms.

In producing themselves, such beings as the ascidian tunicates and oppossum shrimp have opted for the rarest of materials. With them and their "expensive tastes," living sculpture has been raised to a fine art.

The development of modern art even parallels a trend in biomineralization. The nautilus is a "living fossil" related to the squid and octopus. Its ancestors were once much more prevalent in the world's oceans. The nautilus has a powerful aragonite "beak" capable of crushing bones. Its shell is also aragonite, while its balancing organ is formed of calcite; in addition, it has normal "kidney stones" formed of shelly phosphate minerals.

The nautilus and its descendants illustrate biomineralization as an evolutionary work in progress. The balancing organs in this organism are formed from loose assemblages of crystals in a "pinpoint mineralization." But over evolutionary time this loose polycrystalline network has been sculpted together. In the balancing organs of more recently evolved descendant cephalopods such as octopus and squid, the scattered pinpoint array of crystals has coalesced. All nautilus-type organisms have kidney stones, but in some species the kidney has lost its function. Nonetheless, because the need to make shells is so strong, the kidney stones have been retained. They continue to serve as reservoirs used to store the raw skeletal materials calcium and phosphate within the organism. Like romantic knights of the Middle Ages, in the ancient oceans marine creatures evolved protective armors. They formed poking appendages and rock-cracking jaws to break down coarse or protected foods. But eventually speed substituted for armory. Coy survival ploys such as the ink squirted by the squid and the intelligence of the octopus came into play. Today the squid and the octopus lack shells. They do not biomineralize like their *Nautilus* ancestors. Yet their responsive bodies, and ours, still use calcium to think and react. Calcium crucially mediates in the cell-to-cell interactions thought to be the neurological basis for reflex and reflexive thought. Calcium is lethal to cells in a free ionic state, and although calcium ions are 10,000 times more prevalent in the oceans than is the poison cyanide, calcium itself has been incorporated into the very marrow of life, into its skeletons and shells, and in physiological processes ranging from blood clotting to thinking. When Dali lay down on a Spanish beach to tease forth the image of a woman, when he sketched a nude reclining in a seabed with nothing but pigment and chalk, calcium was making use of *him*.

New Alchemists

Our fish ancestors evolved in the sea, and humanity, through biospherics, could once again return to the sea. Similar to moving to space, underwater habitation could be accomplished through biospheres. With his wife Nancy Jack Todd, John Todd has already brought such technology to the surface if not the bottom of the ocean. In the late 1960s the Todds founded the New Alchemy Institute on Cape Cod in Hatchville, Massachusetts. Whereas the first alchemists were inspired by the goal of transmuting base metals such as lead into precious metals, primarily gold, the new alchemists have far more successfully pursued their goal of transmuting base materials such as spent soil, water, and air into beautiful, edible landscapes. Central to the new alchemy philosophy is that biology be the model of design. Thus, in one of their first "bioshelters," the Todds combined architecture and agriculture inside a transparent geodesic structure that served as the walls of both a greenhouse and a human home. Mirroring the proportion of ocean to land on the surface of the Earth, the Todds had a subsurface pond dug to collect solar radiation and to buffer temperature swings. To mimic the natural nutrient-distributing turbulence of the oceans, the couple introduced mirror carp into their indoor pond; the powerful movements of these fish economically ensured that the warm surface waters were mixed with the cooler underlayers. To filter the water, a task accomplished by the great blue whales in the oceans at large, the Todds brought in tilapia, edible fish that fed on the algae growing in the pond of the geodesic dome. Finally, to replace rivers in the natural habitat, which carry terrestrial nutrients into the oceans, they added white amur. These fish fed on the grass, flower stalks, and other vegetable matter conveniently available in the indoor garden planted around the ocean. As the Todds say, although this early design has been in many ways superceded, its basic principle, the circling transmutation of cheap materials and wastes into attractive and nutritious life forms, has not.

The architecture at the New Alchemy Institute is an organic extension of the life it contains. In a bioshelter named the Cape Cod Ark, large rocks absorb sunlight and store heat in tall, transparent cylinders of fish and algae. The solar algae ponds, as the cylinders are called, are a module of many New Alchemy designs; the Todds' book, *Bioshelters, Ocean Arks, City Farming*, depicts these slender synthetic ponds integrated into a wide variety of unexpected settings, including vacant lot "bioshelter parks," the sidewalk aligning rows of urban apartments, and even a bus stop.[11] One version of the solar algae tanks, a slender "organ pipe" biodesign, not only acts as a recycling micro-aquaculture farm but also looks attractive. The Todds point out the energetic wastefulness and inappropriateness of structures such as ranch houses and skyscrapers, which have been transplanted to all corners of the Earth regardless of different local conditions. Their own home has been redone to include a southern-exposure greenhouse open to the living room and with fiberglass fish tanks of the slender organ-pipe variety. The cylindrical tanks also behave as passive solar collectors, warming them at night and exemplifying the New Alchemy dictum that the same structure serves multiple functions, as biological structures do. The Todds harvest catfish, trout, tilapia, mussels, oysters, salad greens, tomatoes, herbs, and tangerines from their transmuted dwelling.

If greenhouses are for plants, human-holding dwellings such as these might be called green*homes*. It is the making of a self-sufficient home, an abode or a dwelling place that not only houses but provides for those within it that makes such structures so different from ordinary houses. Upon visiting the New Alchemy Institute, architect Buckminster Fuller told a group of visitors that they were witnessing the way much more of humanity would be living in the future. Gregory Bateson said that New Alchemy represented an "epistemology with a future." Indeed, such abodes with their internal farming may one day be the norm on planet

Earth. Like seeds, environmentally open bioshelters and their closed relatives, biospheres, may be transplanted to pelagic space and to submarine
depths, or to the surface of other planets or inside space stations. Recycling
technology provides humanity with the wherewithal to manufacture, export, and dwell inside ecological oases. The resourceful people of the
small, resource-lacking island of Japan have shown considerable interest
in such designs: indeed, it is possible that the New Alchemy Institute is
already beginning to provide a guide for post-industrial cities—self-reliant
cities that internally recycle their edible landscapes, cities whose vacant
lots and barren rooftops have been transformed into aesthetically arranged
Japanese food gardens, cities as lush in places as the jungle environment
that was humanity's original home and which is, perhaps, still preserved
like a romantic memory by our genes.

In 1981, Nancy and John Todd formed another company, called
Ocean Arks International, which builds inhabitable ocean-going vessels.
Here the inspiration is to build ships of biological hope and design, carrying
on-board greenhouses, and sailing elegantly without excessive dependence
on fossil fuels. This too presages not just a local but a planetary development, which is to say that people may move to the ocean in devices
not unlike these long before our descendants trek en masse to the stars.
Ocean habitations based on biospheric principles may ultimately become
inexpensive and commonplace. As populations grow and as industry and
national economies expand, less and less territory is available on Earth
for human beings to inhabit.

Underwater cities are definitely over the human horizon. Philip Morrison, an MIT physicist, a radio astronomer, and a pioneer organizer of
the search for extraterrestrial intelligence, claims that the next logical step
for our expanding technical civilization will be to adapt to life
underwater—as opposed to outer space, so often discussed, yet so relatively
expensive. Our children may build on or in—or at the bottom of—the
oceans.

At the decline of a civilization, populaces may become interested in
mystery religions, occult ideas, and fringe beliefs. Perhaps the United
States is in such a phase of decline; I once thought a good idea for a best
seller would be a book that locates the lost continent of Atlantis beneath
the Bermuda triangle. Although there is no critical evidence for such
things as Atlantis, the Bermuda triangle, and the Loch Ness sea monster,
they do generate a prodigious paraliterary genre, filling up whole sections

of American bookstores. However dubious the reality of the topics of occult sciences, future technics may literally make them come true. Long before we see a New Earth erected on another planet by spacegoers, we may produce the lost island of Atlantis, not a barnacled ghost town but a thriving, electrically lit metropolis, with ocean-based economies built on biospheric technologies.

CHAPTER 5

~

Pantropy

When we think of settling other planets, we normally envision ourselves staying biologically as we are. But in some science-fiction stories it is not the planetary environment but individual people who are changed. Instead of putting biospheres under the ocean, for example, people might be surgically implanted with an extra layer of blubber or genetically altered to grow gills and breathe water. "Pantropy" is a word coined by science-fiction writer James Blish. It means to "grow everywhere" or "change everything" and refers to humanity technologically altering its members to adapt to a wide variety of once-alien environments.[1] Pantropy stresses the changing of individual organisms. Biospherics, on the other hand, emphasizes the recreating of the environment to which life belongs. In reality both processes occur: as life grows, it encroaches upon new territory, remaking environments into versions of itself. What evolves is not the organism in a given environment, but both together: the organism-and-its-environment as a single entity.

Life arose as stinking muck in shallow ocean. (Due to chemically reduced carbon-sulfur compounds, the biosphere in the Archean Eon must have smelled something like a cesspool, like rotten eggs, decaying fish, and garbage; though, of course, these smells preceded the organisms with which we may associate them today.) But the biosphere has come a long way: witness deep sea divers or space-walking cosmonauts. Nonetheless, human life is still confined to the planetary surface. In the rarified stratosphere organs explode, bursting through the skin. There simply is not enough surrounding pressure to keep one intact as a discrete, skin-encapsulated biological package. (This is why airplanes are pressurized and why opening a cabin door at such high altitudes will bring on suction effects like a vacuum pulling out the airplane's contents.) The pressure inside the body has evolved to match the pressure of the atmosphere impinging at the Earth's surface.

We need protection from pressure changes if we're going to survive in extraterrestrial environments. Some sort of cover or capsule is required to live in the upper reaches of the biosphere; some way is necessary to bring the pressure at the Earth's surface beyond the surface of the Earth. When land plants evolved from marine algae, they devised rigid compounds, such as the cellulose and lignin found in wood to support themselves out of water and waxy compounds to seal their leaves and prevent them from drying out. As amphibians diverged to become reptiles, they produced the thick-shelled and impermeable amniotic egg, encapsulating within a hard coating the watery environment that was "outside" for their ancestors. Is it possible that what we consider as "outside," the nature in which we walk, will be the inside of *our* descendants?

Throughout evolution, organisms have changed both their environments and themselves. As flaccid algae needed a slick waterproof cuticle to live on dry land, so we require the metallic "shell" of a supersonic jet or space vehicle to travel through the stratosphere. As we go into space the distinction between changing the environment to suit life and changing life to suit the environment dissolves. Indeed, it is precisely the movement into a new territory that forces us to reconceptualize our former environment as part of our self.

Vitanova

Geneticist Robert Haynes of York University in Toronto has made some useful distinctions with regard to people playing God and seeding life on other planets. Haynes coined the word "ecopoiesis," which refers to the fabrication upon formerly sterile worlds of viable ecosystems.[2] Haynes distinguishes "ecopoiesis" from "terraformation," a word brought into currency by science fiction that means "making Earthlike." Ecopoiesis is more basic than terraformation because it sets up a sustainable ecosystem that may or may not be capable of supporting human beings. For example, Mars might be seeded with microbes in a specially designated crater or area or over the entire surface. If all of Mars became inhabited by microbes from Earth, they might well set up a sustainable ecosystem without it being inhabitable by animals. It would be harsh, stench-ridden, similar to the Earth in the Hadean or Archean Eons. The Earth was not inhabitable by animals until 2000 million years ago when biological evolution had built up plants on land and oxygen in the atmosphere. Mars seeded with microbes might be ecopoietic and alive but not able to support people until a similar wait. Or Mars, because of its different geology and physical and chemical conditions, might never evolve an oxygen atmosphere on its own but move in different, totally unexpected directions. In Haynes's vocabulary, such a newly lively planetary neighbor might be aptly called "Vitanova."

Nonetheless, under conscious human direction, Mars, already the most Earthlike of all planets, could become "Terranova"—a truly Earthlike terraformed planet with water, an oxygen atmosphere, and all the requisites for people to walk and live in the open on its surface. Although expensive and ethically problematic, such a project would not be impossible for a nation-state. According to Haynes, it would tax our civilization about as much as building the pyramids of Giza cost Egypt or erecting the Great Wall of China cost China: a huge and amazing engineering project, to be sure, but a doable one. Nonetheless, such a project to make Mars Earthlike enough to support humans might take hundreds of thousands of years; it would be something we do for our descendants more than for ourselves.

Although once strictly within the speculative field of science fiction, proposals for warming Mars and changing its chemistry to support carbon-based life have now entered into serious scientific discussion. The proposals range from reflecting light off giant space mirrors to melt the polar space caps, to sprinkling the same poles with dark light-absorbing powders, to introducing halocarbons that act as warming greenhouse gases into the Martian atmosphere. These proposals have many practical snags, of course: space mirrors will melt Martian ice caps, yes, but the ice caps then will recondense at lower latitudes in a solid phase; seasonal dust storms on Mars would block the heat-absorbing qualities of black powder; introducing halocarbons into the atmosphere would be prohibitively expensive, requiring far more rocketships for delivery than the combined arsenals of the superpowers. More radical suggestions include fertilizing Mars by importing compounds from beyond the asteroid belt and blowing craters in the Martian surface to mimic Earth's atmospheric pressures.[3]

Panspermia

The question of biogenesis on Mars raises questions about our own origins. According to Francis Crick, codiscoverer of DNA, life on Earth began not by evolving here but by being seeded from elsewhere. This is an update of the ancient doctrine of "panspermia." In the fifth century B.C., Greek philosopher Anaxagoras held that resistant "ethereal germs" abounded in the cosmos and grew when they came into contact with the "slimy earth," the fertile ground of this celestial body. Crick's update is even spookier, since he suggests that it is no accident that life originated on planet Earth but that life was consciously planted here in seed form by an extraterrestrial civilization. Despite his prominence, Crick may well be off in his hypothesis of directed panspermia; most origins-of-life scientists believe in the hypothesis of "abiogenesis"—that life arose naturally from nonlife, with no directing influence either divine or extraterrestrial. Organic compounds, while found in space, can be generated in more complex forms, more directly resembling life from simple precursors in the laboratory. It seems more logical to believe that life evolved from nonlife on Earth than to postulate that life came from life in space.

On the other hand, we see again a striking example of something that looks, on the face of it, like unsupported science fiction being, from a slightly different slant, already all too true. For if directed panspermia, the starting of life on distant worlds, does not apply to extraterrestrials, it certainly may apply to terrestrials. We ourselves may start evolution up on Mars and perhaps even all the planets of the solar system before this eon is over.

Creatures of the Supermarket

Believe it or not, there are green photosynthetic worms (species name: *Convoluta roscoffensis*) that do not fit neatly into the classification "animal," as they do not eat through their mouths but simply harvest the gardens that grow within their bodies. Green swimming unicells such as *Euglena* also exist and cannot be classified into either of our two favorite living kingdoms. Indeed, no microbe is really a plant or an animal, nor are any fungi, such as bread mold, or truffles, or morels, or the yeasts that ferment beer. These organisms never were plants, though the realization has only recently been formalized by biology in a new taxonomy of five kingdoms. (Some argue, on the basis of genetic evidence alone, that there are only three kingdoms—two for primitive and recent bacteria and one for all other organisms.) The five kingdoms of life can be represented by an upright outstretched hand, each finger representing a separate kingdom, with the oldest organisms at the bottom, near the wrist. Bacteria, the first kingdom of life to evolve, are represented by the thumb. Some forms of bacteria come together to make the next kingdom of life, the protoctists, represented by the little finger, which consist of organisms whose cells have nuclei. These evolve into fungi, plants, and animals— represented by the ring, index, and middle fingers, respectively. Members of all five kingdoms survive today.[4]

When the world was still considered flat, imaginative Europeans wrote bestiaries and travelogues detailing the existence of bizarre creatures in remote regions. These were mythical animals: some were pictured with several heads or many feet; others combined the limbs and parts of several species into a single body. Those who reported seeing the animals convinced people of their existence, even as some today believe in Bigfoot, the Abominable Snowman, and space aliens. Perhaps there is a romantic strain in all of us that craves the fantastic, the bizarre, and the unbelievable. But we need not have feverish imaginations to find ourselves in the presence of the bizarre. We need only look in a mirror. As it turns out, we ourselves are "chimeras"—that is, we are live mixtures, combining different sorts of creatures and their assorted traits. The creatures we combine are not animals but ancient strains of bacteria. Remnants of at least two and perhaps three different strains have left their genetic traces in virtually every one of the human body's estimated 10 trillion cells.

Evolutionary biologists as eminent as Stephen Jay Gould have repeated that the branches on the tree of life—the traditional spatial representation of evolutionary development, with early life at the bottom and recent forms branching out at the top—never anastomose, that is never join again once having branched out. But it is a mistake to think that organisms only speciate, branch out, and diverge. At crucial points in evolution, the limbs of the evolutionary tree have rejoined; they have converged, bringing together different creatures. The nucleated cell itself, the basic module of animal life throughout our planet, resulted from such convergent speciation: some of the most successful organisms in the entire annals of evolution have been formed from alliances—encounters that began casually with the sharing of food but then evolved into inseparable partnerships. All animal cells contain mitochondria that bear genetic sequences unmistakably tying them to bacterial relatives outside our body. There is little doubt that ancestral cells were invaded by pathogenic aerobic bacteria, whereas others, eaten by larger forms, were not digested but continued living inside their culinary captors. The bacteria set up house, so to speak, inside the invaded lands and have now become as indispensable as the natives. Today the genes of different forms of bacteria are mixed in each of your cells. This intimacy among *different* species is not only more common and longer-lasting in evolution than in sexual genetic union, but it has had a far greater evolutionary impact.

Human civilization could never have occurred without agriculture and domestication. But this process did not begin with humans. Rather, humans and all plants and animals have been formed by such symbioses. Symbiosis is living together; in the case of endosymbiosis, the partnership occurs within the same body.

Recent genetic studies confirm that the cells of all plants and animals contain remnants (mitochondria and chloroplasts) of distinct kinds of bacteria. We may consider our bodies, on the cellular level, to be similar to the dragons of medieval bestiaries: as animals, we have combined the physical and biochemical traits of two and possibly three powerful strains of ancient bacteria. Our bodies are the work of different kinds of microbial life.

In different combinations, these ancient kinds of microbial life united to form the first animal and animal-like cells. Many of the elements used by life are thought to be formed only in the tremendous natural nuclear explosions known as supernovas. The most abundant and biologically important elements in us, such as carbon, nitrogen, and oxygen, are generated in red giant stars. Star stuff, the elements of which our bodies are composed, literally come from space. Stranger than the sensationalist tabloid accounts of dogs abducted by extraterrestrials or men giving birth to chimpanzees are the realizations obtained from contemplating the combined evidence of astrophysics and molecular biology. The first discipline teaches us that our bodies are from space, the second that we are composed of cellular aliens. In a real sense we are all of us "space aliens." I force the terms a bit to make a point. Someone reading these words out of context might rightly be puzzled at this effort to boil down thousands of pages of research into the sorry phrasing of a tabloid headline. My motive is simply to show that checkout-counter sensationalism could equally well apply to the facts of life on Earth as we know them. There is no need to lie to conjure up a sense of the strange. And, as long as we are on the subject of sensational journalism, here is my rendering of the subject of this book into a headline suitable for a tabloid: "Top scientists say, 'Earth alive, on verge of multiple birth!' " How's that for catering to the gossip mongerers?

The Camel

Tabloids aside, to understand the idea of biospheric genesis, it is crucial to understand the community nature of all biological entities, even the most familiar and ordinary. Organisms are adapted not to inert, still-life environs but to living surroundings, an active environment of metabolizing organisms. We dwell in houses, which if made of wood are transformed trees. Inside us live microbes for which we are the environment. Each habitation itself contains a community of interacting organisms whose metabolic wastes and continuous transformation of the environment leads to a sort of dynamic harmony in which biota and environment, living being and home, can never be completely separated.

Different environmental conditions—such as more or less rainfall, varying degrees of sunlight, and soil nutrient composition—translate into sharply different communities of organisms. Although we take them for granted, the natural communities of the biosphere are quite sophisticated. In many cases they seem to be more sophisticated, though unconsciously so, than those made by human designers, be they architects, scientists, or engineers. For example, desert termite mounds, huge cones or pyramids that look like sand castle drippings, are oriented in coordination with the Earth's magnetic field. The mounds are so constructed that the sun at its highest, hottest point hits their narrowest part, away from the broad side where the insects live. Some termites living in arid parts of Africa "air-condition" their hills, achieving an internal relative humidity of 98 per-cent. Termite mounds are constructed from fecal matter and saliva—"found" materials—pasted together to make a brick and mortarlike sub-stance. Not unlike the mud buildings made by nearby humans, the mounds are organic solutions to constraints of the local environment; both regulate temperature better than superficially more advanced concrete houses, which, when exposed to the sun, quickly become hotter inside than even the scorching desert around them.

Unlike most animals, some desert mice and locusts retain and reuse the water formed chemically by respiration. Such water-recycling "tech-nology" is epitomized by camels, who do not urinate ammonia, a usual end product of protein metabolism, but, rather, with the help of symbiotic bacteria living in their maw, recycle it back to form valuable proteins. In most mammals ammonia is excreted as urea with water in the urine. The "individual" camel, however, is not an individual at all. It is a collection, a community of interdependent organisms. Indeed, all organisms on Earth from gnats to elephants bear this multiple nature. The only organisms that could be considered as singular, as monads, are bacteria. But even this evaluation would be wrong since bacteria in nature work together, digesting detritus, emitting gases, altering the chemical composition of the atmosphere and oceans on a global scale.

While mammals who do not pass ammonia in their urine can die of uremia, the "community" we recognize as "a camel" recycles up to 95 percent of its nitrogen, using the nitrogen of this "waste" compound to replace DNA, RNA, and protein molecules. Because the camel recycles its nitrogen, it needs a ration of only one-twentieth the protein from food it would otherwise require. At the same time, since the maw bacteria recycle urea, there is no need to flush away ammonia and water, a very valuable desert resource. The camel survives the harsh environs of the desert by its recirculating physiology.[5]

For life to survive in space a similar ruse is required, an extraterrestrial circulation of Earth life that nonetheless remains almost intrauterine in its egglike circulation and transformation of wastes within technological "shells." We must rethink our relationship to waste matter to move into space. In the extraterrestrial environment it becomes blatantly obvious that excess—whether metabolic, industrial, or technological—must not simply be disposed of but reworked into the cycle of existence. In a sense, we humans as a whole represent an excess on the biogeological face of nature: some of our technological products have been resistant to absorption by the biosphere. The challenge for us is to come up to the biosphere around and within us and to become fully involved in the ancient systems of biospheric circulation. Not man or humanity but the flowing whole of transhuman, multispecies, *biospheric* individuality becomes the measure of all things.

Life is chimerical. As the biosphere exhibits some of the characteristic traits of a single organism, so the individual is both an aggregate of organisms and a part of an aggregation. The organisms comprising individual plant and animal cells and bodies were not originally, nor are they still in many cases, of the same type. The ancestral bacteria may have even been hostile—invading and eating each other before establishing various degrees of tolerance, harmony, and disharmony. But over time, odd couples—and *ménages à trois*, foursomes, and still higher numbered partnerships—triumphed.

Above and beyond the dissonant notes of competition and exlusion, the history of the Earth plays a melody of companionship and compromise. No one denies that life is a struggle to exist. We are always too many. Yet all those we call alive have already resolved or are in the midst of resolving their struggles. Humanity, too, so long seemingly apart from nature and developing on its own technological track, must rise to biospheric standards. From the viewpoint of long-term evolution, it seems incontestable that we must ground ourselves and our products in the ancient ways of Earth life if we are to survive. As a global civilization we must fall in with nature as one would fall in love.

Janus

The biosphere may be, as Lewis Thomas puts it, "the biggest organism in the solar system." But the biosphere is neither animal nor plant. Earth seems to exhibit less order and less topological symmetry than an octopus, an orangutan, or a sunflower. Perhaps "looking out" of the "organism" in which we dwell distorts our view of its overall organization. By contrast, astronauts gazing at Earth from orbit see the planet as a whole. They realize that our concepts of time and space depend on the rotation of the Earth and the gravity of its surface. Viewing the Earth from above, an out-of-body experience occurs. In space, both day and night and up and down disappear into a larger perspective that encompasses the Earth as a whole. Astronauts in orbit can no more see individual animals on the terraqueous surface of the globe than a person at a cocktail party can detect an amoeba floating on another's eye. Stepping back allows one distance, the distance to see what one was and to define what one is.

The idea that a person is a multispecies assemblage extends outward to our connection with the entities that include *us* in *their* organization. Your cells and tissues have bacteria and viruses living in and on them; batallions of fungi, roundworms, and pinworms are normal inhabitants of healthy skin. The stomach and intestines contain immense crowds of yeasts and bacteria—"germs" that not only help digest food but provide trace nutrients and vitamins such as B_5 and folic acid that "we" could not produce without "them." As microbiologist Folsome reminds us, if your animal cells could be magically made to disappear . . .

What would remain would be a ghostly image, the skin outlined by a shimmer of bacteria, fungi, round worms, pin worms and various other microbial inhabitants. The gut would appear as a densely packed tube of anaerobic and aerobic bacteria, yeasts, and other microorganisms. Could one look in more detail, viruses of hundreds of kinds would be apparent throughout all tissues. We are far from unique. Any animal or plant would prove to be a similar seething zoo of microbes.[6]

This multiplex structure also applies to animal communities and societies as well as to the biosphere as an interliving whole.

English philosopher Herbert Spencer wrote that

The social organism, discrete instead of concrete, asymmetrical instead of symmetrical, sensitive in all its units instead of having a single sensitive centre, is not comparable to any particular type of individual organism, animal or vegetal. All kinds of creatures are alike in so far as each exhibits co-operation among its components for the benefit of the whole.[7]

Spencer's statement of the nonanimal, nonplant nature of societies is even more applicable to the biosphere. The biosphere is symbiotic, chimerical, and self-producing. It is not a plant or an animal. It is more like a giant spherical "planimal," an organized network of interdependent, interacting organisms, a superorganism of mysterious affinity and unknown taxonomy. Until recently, it has been one of a kind.

The Earth's biosphere may appear to have less individuality than a person, not because it is any less an autonomous system than we are but simply because it is so unlike us. The imperfect individualism of the Earth's biosphere is due to our unfamiliarity with it or to our inability to conceptualize what is so much greater than we. Perhaps the relative lack of individuality seen in the biospheric "individual," compared to the human "individual," results from the biosphere's actually being less individualized, less autonomous, than we are. Perhaps the biosphere is not yet a distinct individual but is heading in that direction.

If the Earth's biosphere is not symmetrical, as topographically distinct, or as organized as we have come to associate with the term "organism," perhaps such disarray results from its Herculean size: with less evolutionary time at its disposal, the Earth's biosphere simply hasn't yet had the opportunity to consolidate into anything as organized, regular, or topologically symmetrical as a plant or an animal. If this surmise is correct, then you can expect the biosphere to display increasingly more individuality and to behave increasingly more like a recognizable organism.

Arthur Koestler coined the term "holons" to mean parts that are also wholes.[8] In this terminology humanity can be described as one holon nested or nestled within another, the biosphere. Friction arises between the two holons. Like the god Janus, the image of whom Koestler used to explain his antireductionist concept, the holon has two faces. In the dual orientation of the holon, one face looks inward toward the parts that compose the holon, while the other face peers outward at what it partially comprises. The concept of "holonomy" may prove more useful and fruitful than its more common counterpart of autonomy. As human beings we are not alone but at best semiautonomous, integrated into the holonomy of a biosphere of nested hierarchies and networks of interacting, ecologically interwoven and interweaving organisms. Humanity is not a whole but a holon, or as I prefer, a (w)hole. Unable to pin it down, we must allow this indeterminate meaning to linger vibrating a while, oscillating with possibilities, as befits its subject.

CHAPTER 6

~

Overhistory

We cannot lightly dismiss the possibility that the biosphere as an organism may "need" only a certain quantity of human beings. If the surface of the Earth behaves as a physiological system, unfettered human growth may elicit a retaliatory response against the ecologically offending party. For example, burning fossil fuels could raise the mean global temperature by adding carbon dioxide to the atmosphere. As the temperature rises, polar ice caps could break and melt into the oceans, and the sea level would rise. Some of the most populous areas—such as London, New York, and Los Angeles—could be flushed away. Whether one wants to speak of the biosphere as "desiring" it or not, if this occurs the planet will have acted as if it were ridding itself of excess humanity. As a physiological system, the Earth will have "holonomously" reacted to maintain conditions more like those prevailing before the appearance of globally intrusive humanity.

All human history is part of the history of Earth, which is a geophysiological "overhistory": the chronicle of a single living being. Czech novelist Milan Kundera writes of human bias in history, wistfully suggesting that the migration of a given population of birds from one city to another ranks in importance along with European power struggles but is ignored because it is not human. Is this only the flip suggestion that history should be for the birds? Or is he saying that in focusing on the traditional human history of statues, wars, and kings, we have overlooked something far more important, the living history of the biosphere? Lovelock's second Gaia book, *Ages of Gaia*, describes the uncanny persistence with which the peacocks dwelling about his English country home gather together and lay their smelly droppings on the pavement outside the door. At first, he said, he used to curse them, but then it occurred to him that those "ecologically minded birds were doing their best to turn the dead concrete of the path back to living soil again. What better way to digest away the concrete than by daily application of nutrients and bacteria in the shedding of their shit?"[1]

In the past people have not chronicled the history of other species, but now we are being forced to pay closer attention; green politics, conservation movements, and environmental concerns clearly show that the history of the human species is converging with the histories of other species and of the biosphere as a whole. Epochal changes in biospheric organization may have occurred when organisms evolved that, after a period of disruption and adjustment, *enhanced* the functioning of the biosphere. For example, a subtle shift in biospheric organization may have reinforced the evolution of birds (from reptiles). It is difficult to understand how any species or, more generally, any kind of organism can become exceedingly widespread unless it infiltrates the biospheric organization of all organisms. Humanity as a superabundant species producing toxins and, in general, meddling, may be at a certain historical crossroads where our numbers either will or will not be tolerated. For our presence to be tolerated by the biosphere in current (5 billion) or even greater numbers may require that we involve ourselves in the overall life of this planet to a far greater extent than we are doing now. No matter how adept an organism is at propagating itself, if it does not become involved in the life cycles of others, it will fail. And the human requirement to become integrated into the biospheric system becomes critical as our presence becomes felt in the planetary environment.

To explore how we might "become integrated in the biospheric system" and perpetuate our survival, consider the evolution of birds: precisely their waste may have insured them longevity. Coming from reptilian progenitors, birds could have precipitated an improvement in the cycling of an element vital to the biospheric individual: phosphorus. Birds may have biochemically "pushed" the biosphere, increasing global metabolism.

For a long time now there has been what amounts to a "phosphorus crisis" in the biosphere. Although it ranks twelfth in abundance among the elements in the Earth's crust, phosphorus appears mostly in the biologically unavailable form of minerals such as apatite, wavellite, and vivianite. Nonetheless, phosphate ions present in fluids within living tissues are needed by all organisms. Neither DNA nor RNA can be made without phosphorus. The element usually comprises on the average only 0.000009 percent of seawater; this low concentration derives in part from the mad scramble of marine organisms to get the element when it is available as phosphate salts. The chronic shortage of phosphorus imposes an absolute limit on the abundance of life in shallow waters. Upwelling areas where deep ocean water comes to the surface often support rich concentrations of life. The richness in life in these areas is due largely to the supply of phosphorus from dark waters where, in the form of a submarine rain of falling algal skeletons, it gradually accumulates. Taken out of circulation by the death of algae, the phosphorus floats with their tiny shells to the sea floor, limiting other organisms that would grow if only they had access to the element. Upwelling brings this vital resource back to the surface.

Phosphorus is needed to make not only DNA, but also other compounds crucial for the storage and transfer of energy and information in lining cells. But phosphorus cannot be assimilated by cells as apatite. Unlike other nutrient elements needed by life, stores of phosphorus on Earth are rare. Virtually the sole exceptions are the presence of phosphorus in some meteorites and in Cambrian and late Proterozoic phosphorite deposits. Unlike bioelements such as oxygen and nitrogen, phosphorus is never found in a volatile or gaseous form that can waft through the global circulatory system that is the atmosphere. Confronted with the biospheric immobility of phosphorus, organisms have long been in a position similar to that of Tantalus in Greek mythology: they are up to their chins in water with fruit suspended overhead but whenever they bend the water dries up and whenever they reach for the fruit the wind blows the branch out of reach.

Birds may have alleviated this biospheric shortage by doing something often advocated in the human realm: they improved not the quantity of food but the means of distribution. Answering nature's call in the air, birds may have become biospheric messengers. Bird droppings—a major component of which is biologically assimilable phosphorus—long ago spread phosphorus on a global scale. Organisms were no longer tantalized by their inability to get at their food.

The other ways phosphorus travels long distances is as freight carried by swimming or crawling animals or by microbial spores floating hap-hazardly in the winds. With the appearance of migrating birds, the equiv-alent to a biospheric proposal for phosphorus overnight express mail had been put on the table: phosphorus was deployed, transported, and deliv-ered; it was spread thin despite its refractory nature through the circulating atmosphere. Guano mounds on the islands off Peru may be thirty-five meters thick; sea birds and even bats transport it through the air—giving the slow moving element "wings." Could seasonal bird migrations serve a relatively precise function of biospheric phosphorus distribution? Mi-gratory fish such as salmon that swim upstream many hundreds of miles to breed may behave similarly in terms of helping distribute globally scarce but vital geochemicals. This is not to say that fish and birds evolved in order to transport phosphorus. Yet their serendipitous status as atmospheric couriers may render them integral to biospheric physiology in its present form—not as crucial but playing a similar role to hemoglobin molecules delivering oxygen via blood in the human body.

Unstable Atmosphere

Termites may also play a role in the biospheric "holonomy." The equivalent of one-third of the matter grown by plants each year is devoured by wood-eating termites and moves through their insides; much of this matter becomes the atmospheric gas methane. Does methane have a "purpose" in the global body?

Methane in the Earth's atmosphere reacts with oxygen to make carbon dioxide and water. According to Lovelock, the atmosphere is as actively regulated and organized as the skin of our bodies. Indeed, in the late 1960s, before the United States Viking mission to Mars, Lovelock stated that life's absence could be detected on Mars simply by viewing the at-mosphere. When a ray of light pierces a prism it forms a spectrum; the composition of gases in the atmosphere of a planet will form different spectra. Lovelock held that since the gases in the Martian atmosphere as viewed spectrometrically from the Earth were conspicuously normal or in chemical equilibrium, there was no need to fly to Mars to conclude that life did not exist there. Later, after the two Viking spacecraft landed in June and August of 1976, other scientists came to the same conclusion. The Martian probes dropped down on the soil of Mars, took pictures, picked up the soil for analysis with a special scoop, and performed a series of experiments specifically designed to find life. The sensors found that the Martian surface didn't even contain trace quantities of the organic compounds associated with life, let alone life. At least judging from the top twenty centimeters of soil analyzed by the landers' apparatus, Mars was dead.

Meanwhile, Lovelock was developing a different view of Earth life and atmosphere. Contrary to conventional geologists who viewed life as a passenger on Earth, Lovelock believes that life totally infiltrates a planet's surface.

> [If] you have life on a planet, it is bound to use any of the mobile media that are available to it, like the atmosphere or the oceans, as a source of raw materials and also as a conveyor belt for getting rid of waste products and so on. And such a use of the atmosphere— and there wasn't an ocean on Mars, there's only an atmosphere— will be bound to change its chemical composition away from that of a lifeless planet.[2]

Lovelock holds that life, a planetary phenomenon, must involve the atmosphere.

Strikingly different from Mars and Venus, both of which have atmospheric compositions that make sense to a chemist familiar with how gases react in the laboratory, the atmosphere of our Earth contains gases such as oxygen and methane that react violently together and so should vanish to be replaced by other, chemically expected compounds (such as carbon dioxide and water). Yet, here on Earth, these reactive gases remain in each other's company over geological time. Oxygen, for example, can be deduced from charcoal in the fossil record. (Somewhat uncannily, life leaves fossil traces in the rock record with the same materials—namely, chalk and charcoal—that an art student uses to draw a live figure on a piece of paper.) The charcoal shows up in the rocks regularly for at least the last 300 million years. Now, if oxygen in the atmosphere were less than 15 percent, no match or lightning would ever start a fire. So oxygen must have been at higher concentrations than that. But if oxygen had been at higher concentrations than 25 percent, worldwide fires would burn so wildly that evidence of ancient forests would have been obliterated. Evidence of fossil forests abounds, however, so the reactive gas oxygen has remained in our atmosphere for hundreds of millions of years in the proportion of about 21 percent—even though it reacts violently with the hydrogen-rich carbon compounds characteristic of life. In a way, our planet now resembles a giant battery, kept energetic and continually re-charged by the sun. Looking around the solar system, it is clearly a chemical anomaly, a space oddity.

Lovelock posits that the Earth's atmospheric composition, its mean surface temperature, the pH and salt concentration of the world's oceans—as well as many other physical factors—are under active bio-logical control. According to one line of thought, the hospitability of the environment over geological time is a coincidence; if we had not been lucky in terms of the inanimate processes stabilizing our planetary envi-ronment, we would not be around to coo over life's physiological control of the Earth's surface. But Earth without life would look as barren as the moon; clearly, life is deeply involved in geological processes in the would-be "inanimate" environment. Anti-Gaia scientists may accept this weak form of Gaia—Gaia as integration of biology and geology, Earth and life; but they reject the strong form—Gaia as a unified life form keeping itself fit on a planetary scale. This latter they call mysticism.

It is worth noting that to speak about anything we must use metaphors; therefore, Lovelock's penchant for describing Gaia in colorful, meta-phorical language should not be used to dismiss Gaia. It is also worth noting that human consciousness and purposefulness is itself—in the eyes of the same hard-nosed scientists who would dismiss Gaia—the result of the blind forces of mutation and natural selection. For Lovelock, the global environment self-maintains; the world around us, like the flesh and blood of our bodies, is physiologically attuned to itself. Yet over its long history, in Lovelock's view, the Earth has evolved through discrete phys-iochemical phases, ages in the growth of a planetary being. The accu-mulation of the dangerous energetic gas oxygen in the atmosphere marks the transition from one age of the Earth to the other. Such a violent transition might seem incompatible with Lovelock's idea of global regu-lation, yet each of us at puberty undergoes a similarly drastic change from an ancient to a new regime. An anaerobic Earth, one lacking in oxygen, marks the early period of our planet's youth. On Earth, it will never come again.

* * *

Although the earliest records from rocks show an absence of oxygen, it is clear from oxidized metals that roughly 2 billion years ago some oxygen had accumulated in the atmosphere. While the anaerobic life that inhabited the planet until then must have been killed off in droves, the reactive nature of oxygen that made it so dangerous also created an opportunity that life makes use of today. Originally, oxygen destabilized the ancient regime; today it has settled to form about one-fifth of the atmosphere. Because it is very reactive, oxygen provides animals such as ourselves with the power to do things such as walk, talk, and read.

But what has all this got to do with termites? Well, termites occur over about two-thirds of the Earth's land surface; there may be as many as three-quarters of a ton of termites for every person in the world. Moreover, termites convert roughly 1 percent of the carbon in wood into methane in the atmosphere. Since methane may be necessary to stabilize the atmospheric level of oxygen, and since termites produce so much "natural gas," they may be playing a crucial role in the "physiology" of the Earth. If extraterrestrials knew much about life they might be able to tell there were termites here—and cows, whose guts are full of methanogenic bacteria—simply by the abnormal quantities of methane in an oxidizing atmosphere that should quickly destroy the gas. As much as half the methane in the atmosphere may be produced by termites. In summary, termites may—like birds—be so successful because they help not only themselves but the Earth as a living body. They juggle the atoms that comprise the chemically unstable system of the atmosphere, the biosphere's circulatory system.

Planetary Drugging

As the example of methane shows, garbage never goes "out" but only "around." Similarly, our human wastes—not so much sewage as industrial exhaust from pesticides to radioactive waste—may one day play a role in biospheric functioning or development. Industrial wastes pressure the biosphere and may prompt a change of regime as drastic and as dramatic as the switch to an oxygen-rich atmosphere. Everything that we create technologically must either stockpile or come into biological circulation.

Obviously—as Rachel Carson documented in her landmark report *Silent Spring*—much of it *is* coming into circulation. The eggs of Siberian birds and other organisms seemingly removed from our polluting activities nonetheless carry man-made toxins in their bodies and young. If the planet is a living body then it can be pharmacologically affected. Perhaps the biosphere is, in effect, being drugged. At this point it would be presumptuous to say whether such drugging is helpful or harmful to people. Like antibiotics, the chemicals we introduce could act as a poison or as a cure. Perhaps the strangest idea is that the dose is *naturally* upsetting and *as a whole* similar to the flood of hormones during puberty and adolescence: disruptive to the point of depression and possibly even suicide—or, in the case of the biosphere, "biocide"—the wholesale destruction of species we might expect from a nuclear war. Yet, who among us, having become an adult, would wish to return to childhood? The painful drugging, this planetary moodiness, may be normal, necessary, a rite of passage.

In the long run, organisms probably do not endure if they do not fit into the functioning of the biosphere. There is every chance in the world that the geophysiology is primary to, and more powerful than, anything we can say about it. All our analogies are in terms of our bodies, ourselves; yet these bodies are themselves mere structures in the grammar or syntax of a biospheric language of organismic interaction that transcends human meaning. We are punctuation points in a planetary overhistory that will be written in numerous forms, in numerous ways, and not only by people.

Life on Earth forms such a complex whole that any analysis of it is bound to be insufficient, if not riddled with inconsistencies. The biosphere contains, or consists of (depending on how you look at it) some 30 million "species" of living organisms. Our own species has some 5 billion members and many species have more. Indeed, species are counted differently by different biologists so no official census has been commissioned. Nonetheless, clearly there are far more life forms than have been identified and described in scholarly journals. Even our own kingdom, the animal, contains incestuous mites, microscopic burrowers, and red tube worms that live at the bottom of the sea. We share membership in the same phylum with didemnids—green, lemon-shaped animals bathing in the Pacific ocean. This is the chordate phylum. But there are over fifty phyla of animals alone. All the familiar animals from beavers to snakes and giraffes belong with us in the same chordate subphylum of animals with backbones. Consider the other four kingdoms, with all their classes, phyla, subphyla, and species, and one realizes that our ignorance of the biosphere's anatomy is exceeded only by our ignorance of its physiology— including the possibility that it has, like us, a neuropsychology, a "mind." In the end, we have only one living planet. In many ways, it is beyond compare.

CHAPTER 7

~

One Blood

Harvard University geochemist Heinrich Holland on National Public Radio stated that the Gaia hypothesis is excessive and unneeded. If life were put through a giant blender and spread out over the surface of the Earth, he said, it would make a film like that of peanut butter in a peanut butter sandwich; his point was that the mass of life is so negligible at the Earth's surface it could have, at the most, very little effect. Such a statement seems to rely on what is almost a caricature of modern science: the reduction of everything to quantities and quantities alone. But pharmacologically the same quantity may not be equal: a sailor may take 500 milligrams of vitamin C and prevent himself from getting scurvy; a teenager may take 500 micrograms of LSD and jump out of a window in ontological frustration. These, too, are negligible quantities, but their impacts are a matter of life and death. The role of organisms on the surface of the Earth cannot be gauged by their weight; organisms continually sense, amplify, and alter the chemistry of their surrounding environments. The power of organisms is not a simple function of their size or weight, any more than our bodies conform to the simple shapes of Euclidean geometry.

In a *Toronto Star* newspaper column, arms expert Gwynne Dyer predicts that the Gaia hypothesis will become the basis for a new planetary religion in the coming millennium. Writes Dyer:

Whether or not there ever turns out to be scientific evidence for a single, co-ordinated global living entity of which all species and individuals are essentially components, it is as metaphor that the Gaean [sic] hypothesis has such a promising future.

Gaea is tailor-made for a late industrial society that will have to come to grips, over the next couple of generations, with problems that range from pollution control of every kind and the need to accept resource constraints to potentially severe climatic and environmental change. It gives a name, a purpose and even a kind of personality to the ecosphere [sic] that we must preserve for our own good.

To create mass political support for new forms of policy and behavior, you need to present them as a coherent and accessible package of simple ideas (especially if they require a radical break with traditional attitudes). And what will be needed most of all, in the coming decades, is a simple package that unifies all the various ecological concerns from the ozone layer to the rain forests.[1]

A peanut butter sandwich or a living planet—which shall we choose? Part of the problem for scientists is that the notion of planetary physiology brings old "nonscientific" cosmologies of an animate Earth, traces of which can be found even (or especially) in the Old Testament, to the fore, just as the radical findings of modern physics cast a new, confirming light on some of the ancient dicta of Eastern philosophy. As a geophysiological, if unconscious, being, the Earth may nonetheless be more complex and coordinated than our wildest dreams.

Chief Seattle

Native peoples of North America traditionally hold that the Earth, in all its parts, is alive. The famous Suquamish Chief Seattle commented, for example, that all is connected by a single blood:

The shining water that moves in the streams and rivers is not just water, but the blood of our ancestors. . . . Each ghostly reflection in the clear water of the lakes tells of events and memories in the life of my people. The water's murmur is the voice of my father's father.

The rivers are our brothers. They quench our thirst. They carry our canoes and feed our children. So you must give to the rivers the kindness you would give any brother.

If we sell you our land, remember that the air is precious to us, that the air shares its spirit with all the life it supports. The wind that gave our grandfather his first breath also receives his last sigh. The wind also gives our children the spirit of life. So if we sell you our land, you must keep it apart and sacred, as a place where man can go to taste the wind that is sweetened by meadow flowers.

Will you teach your children what we have taught our children? That the earth is our mother? What befalls the earth, befalls all the sons of the earth.

This we know: The earth does not belong to man, man belongs to earth. All things are connected like the blood which unites us all. Man did not weave the web of life, he is merely a strand in it. Whatever he does to the web, he does to himself.

One thing we know: Our god is also your god. The earth is precious to him and to harm the earth is to heap contempt on its creator.

Your destiny is a mystery to us. What will happen when the buffalo are all slaughtered? The wild horses tamed? What will happen when the secret corners of the forest are heavy with the scent of many men and the view of the ripe hills is blotted with talking wires? Where will the thicket be? Gone! Where will the eagle be? Gone! And what is it to say goodbye to the swift pony and the hunt? The end of living and the beginning of survival.

When the last Red Man has vanished with his wilderness, and his memory is only the shadow of a cloud moving across the prairie, will these shores and forests still be here? Will there be any of the spirit of my people left?

We love this earth as a newborn loves its mother's heartbeat. So, if we sell you our land, love it as we have loved it. Care for it as we have cared for it. Hold in your mind the memory of the land as it is when you receive it. Preserve the land for all children and love it, as God loves us all.

As we are part of the land, you too are part of the land. This earth is precious to us. It is also precious to you. One thing we know: There is only one God. No man, be he Red Man or White Man can be apart. We *are* brothers after all.

So Chief Seattle answered in 1852 to a presidential requirement to sell his lands: "The President in Washington sends word that he wishes to buy our land. But how can you buy or sell the sky? The land? The idea is strange to us. If we do not own the freshness of the air and the sparkle of the water, how can you buy them?"[2]

Eastern religions have also focused on a oneness of nature. Buddhists, for instance, do not believe there is any distinction between subject and object, so that for them a living cosmos implies oneness. In the West, too, mystics have had a way of breaking down the subjective barriers of the ego and identifying with their surroundings. This makes it impossible to put a fence up or to erect a border around what lives. The limits of the living are to be found wherever the organism participates in looking.

Historically the view of Earth as alive may have been a rare state of mind, but in the "space age" seeing the Earth as a single ecological entity is becoming increasingly commonplace. What Frank White calls the "overview effect"[3]—the altered state of consciousness of looking at the Earth from space reported in some form by almost all astronauts—is filtering down to us here on Earth. Someday we may all be able to take Polaroid snapshots on a weekend jaunt to the moon. But even a black-and-white newspaper photo of the planet gives us a perspective of the outside that we remember when we lie down on the grass on a clear blue day and gaze upward at the clouds. We know now that this is not the only view, but a provincial one. We are *underneath* the clouds, *inside* the membranous atmosphere. The Earth never settles into the physiochemical norm of what would be expected for a lifeless planet of its position and size. It stabilizes gases and regulates atoms to form an atmosphere out of chemical equilibrium. Complex chemical compounds not seen anywhere else in the universe pervade our air. They are as rare and as rich as cosmic jewels. Minute portions may induce massive effects, as when venom from the skin of a toad kills a large animal. Erotic scents called pheromones also bring on powerful effects despite being administered in quantities so minuscule they cannot be seen. The pheromones work not within bodies like hormones but are carried in the space between organisms. In a sense, pheromones are Gaian hormones. For example, drugs from cocaine to alcohol in the body politic cause human societies to behave in distinct ways. If one considers that cells may come together symbiotically to form new organisms, one realizes that pheromones at the individual level of animals may act as hormones at the societal or biospheric levels. By the same token, the making and taking of chemically potent "drugs" by collections of related body cells has led to the intricate systems of biochemical control involving hormones, behavior, and growth.

The atmosphere is a liquid shell the matter of which we breathe and through which we stroll. It is an invisible membrane that we may ignore but from which we cannot detach ourselves. Our breath is the part of us that is recognizably global in its being. Lifeless planets do not have such atmospheric membranes. The word "spirit" comes from the Latin word for breathing, *spiritus*. The atmosphere vividly demonstrates the extent to which life or living organization is not shackled within individual bodies, but resides between and beyond them as well. If a scientist on another star system discovered a means of observing the planets of our solar system, he or she would be able to detect the life of Earth solely by the chemical properties of our atmosphere, as Lovelock did for Mars. Like a tiger cowrie shell glittering in the sunlight of a Hawaiian beach, the organized pattern of our atmospheric shell announces the existence of an organism. We cannot directly perceive the chemical composition of our atmosphere. We have not evolved under circumstances that would make such observation crucial to our survival. Paradoxically, such an interpretation, not only of other life forms but of the life form we are part of, may imminently be crucial to the survival of the human species. The Gaia hypothesis states that the chemistry and temperature of the atmosphere, oceans, and sediments—the surface of the Earth—is under active control by the biota, the organic surface of the Earth. Oxygen accounts for about one-fifth the atmosphere; the mean temperature of the lower atmosphere is about 22°C; and the pH of the planetary surface averages just over 8.0. Evidence from the fossil record shows that these anomalies have persisted for millions of years. That the Earth is alive may be, like many other things in art and science, only a beautiful fiction. But it is fast becoming a necessary one.

Temperature Regulation

The Gaia hypothesis gives an answer to a mystery that has been gnawing at scientists for nearly two decades: the so-called "faint sun paradox." Astrophysical theories of the birth and death of stars uniformly suggest that the sun began 5 billion years ago, smaller than it is now; it progressively increased in size and luminosity by some 30 percent or more. Yet, fossil evidence shows that liquid water, including rivers and lakes, existed at the Earth's surface for the last 3 billion years. Did the biosphere change its temperature as the sun grew in luminosity and the radiation reaching the Earth increased?

The traditional non-Gaian explanation for such temperature control assumes that at best life played an incidental role. Sometimes called the "Goldilocks problem," the question is why Venus became too hot and Mars too cold for life while the Earth remained "just right." One non-Gaian answer to this climatological problem is that these three planets differ in their respective abilities to cycle carbon dioxide between their oceans and atmospheres. Mars, in part because it was relatively small, lost its internal heat, becoming so cold that it could no longer release carbon dioxide from carbonated sediments to replace carbon dioxide leaving the atmosphere in the form of carbonic acid rainfall. Since carbon dioxide was no longer available to let in sunlight and trap it as heat, Mars went into a deep freeze. On Venus, by contrast, there was so much carbon dioxide heating up the planet as infrared radiation that a runaway greenhouse effect arose, creating a hellish planet too hot for life. From this traditional viewpoint, life's happy climate is incidental, a lucky accident of a temperature-regulating carbon dioxide cycle between crust and atmosphere, which was established on Earth but disrupted on Mars and Venus. Life took advantage of, but had nothing to do with, the temperature of the Earth being "just right" for billions of years despite the increasing heat of the sun.

From the Gaian perspective, however, life actively participated in climatological modulation. Many animals regulate their temperature. All animals are evolved multicellular clones. Might not the Earth, as a superorganism containing organisms, regulate itself by feedback processes similar to those at work in a human being made of cells? Honeybees act together to modulate the temperature of their hive and are recognized, along with other social insects, as forming superorganisms. As a single giant superorganism, the Earth, too, would regulate its temperature, chemical composition, and environment in general not through any outside agency but as the aggregate result of the organisms busy within it.

Cyberspace Flowers

Lovelock and coworker Andrew Watson have made mathematical models showing that "Daisyworld"—a computer-generated planet containing black and white daisies, and sometimes cows, foxes, rabbits, evolving viruses, and other species as well—can effectively control its temperature to keep cool despite the increasing luminosity of a nearby sun.[4] Like the real Gaia (which has survived damage from "planetesimals" equivalent to third-degree burns of 60 percent of the skin area of a human fire victim), the Gaian models recover from biological insults, be they viruses from within or meteorites from without. The models, a breathtaking revision of the entire field of theoretical ecology, show that no mystical assumptions need be made for organisms to control features of their environment as a unity: planetary regulation in Daisyworld results quite naturally from the effects upon the environment of individually growing organisms.

As recent work details, in the real world temperature regulation may be accomplished by plankton: to protect themselves plankton called coccolithophores produce dimethyl sulfide, a gas implicated in the genesis and reflectivity of marine stratus clouds. If the plankton grow more when it is hotter, they could well produce more of this gas, leading to more cloud cover and reflection of light and heat into space, consequently cooling the planet like a giant thermostat.[5] A recent article in *Nature*[6] has contested this supposed mechanism of planetary physiology by noting that sulfur dioxide emissions, produced mainly by industry in the developed countries, have not noticably increased cloud cover over the Northern Hemisphere or led to a noticable decrease in Northern Hemisphere temperatures within the last 100 years. Sulfur dioxide is not dimethyl sulfide but is assumed to work similarly. Whether or not this particular mechanism of worldwide temperature control is even partially correct, real temperature regulation of the planet's surface is far more likely to be accomplished by production and consumption of carbon dioxide, methane, and other "greenhouse" gases than it is by simple color changes as in the model. The *Nature* article shows that aspects of the Gaia hypothesis concerning the physiology of the Earth can be tested in the most rigorous way by working scientists. The Daisyworld model works not in reality but in the cyberspace of a computer; and yet it works. The most exciting thing about the Daisyworld model is how it brackets—how it raises and at the same time dismisses—the question of consciousness: the daisies in the model are behaving as if they knew what they were doing, they are not just acting but acting intelligently; yet, this is simply an emergent effect of their collective activities. Does our self-awareness emerge "environmentally" from interacting cells? If so, might not the planet also, in some sense, think?

The Sinews of Atlas

Life's effect upon the Earth's crust is so pervasive that even the great tectonic movements beneath the oceans may be prompted by organismic collectives. Though not yet proven, a series of provocative coincidences suggest that the most apparently inanimate and Herculean geological processes are under biological dominion.

To glimpse how life may be implicated in plate tectonics, consider first that ten times the amount of salt that should be in the ocean isn't there: chemical and physical calculations show that salt should pile up cumulatively in the great marine basins. Since there is no geological escape hatch to remove this salt, we have to assume that *life itself* keeps the oceans free from the high levels of salt that might otherwise accumulate there. Marine creatures cannot tolerate high salt concentrations; they would be poisoned, literally pickled to death, were salt not somehow being removed. But if life forms take the salt, where do they put it? Where does the salt go? How does it get there?

The missing salt is found at the edges of the sea, on coastal lands in evaporite deposits. Evaporites are sand-ridden expanses—flats and fields rich in minerals and salts. Charles Darwin cast his curious eyes over such deposits; we find references to them in his notebooks. We now know that what Darwin saw were packed communities of bacteria. The exudates, the cellular secretions of these beings wrap around particles of salt preventing them from being dissolved again into the water. Such natural salt mining might work to hold vast quantities back from the ocean, but only if the land is broad and flat and in the tropics or subtropics so that sufficient evaporation can take place. With limestone acting as a lubricant, land masses slide over the mantle, slipping especially over stationary sources of tremendous heat coming from within the Earth. The mobile plates tend to accumulate in the tropical and semitropical zones where the slippery limestone was produced. Slipping about, they may create platforms for salt removal in their wake. So, while the details of sifting salt from the oceans remain unclear, ocean salinity is being regulated. Without foresight, but due to the immense continuous growth of microorganisms able to coat salt and thus prevent it from returning to solution in microbial mats and crystalline lagoons, life has evolved to protect its environment, to keep the seas eminently inhabitable, free from becoming a supersaturated vat of poison, suitable for salt curing or pickling but not life.

According to geologist Don Anderson, the transmutation of atmospheric carbon dioxide into calcium carbonate sediment, a chemical reaction for which life is primarily responsible on Earth, could have destabilized crustal rocks so much it began the process of plate tectonics. "[P]late tectonics may exist on the Earth because limestone-generating life evolved here."[7] No plate tectonic processes, responsible for continental drift, have been observed on Mars or Venus.*

Absence of a mechanism is not evidence of absence of a phenomenon. For example, the geographic jig-saw-like fit of Africa into America suggested to Alfred Wegener that they were originally together and had drifted apart. Nobody, however, believed in his "continental drift" until magnetometers were dragged, the mid-Atlantic rift was recognized, and elaborate mechanisms were proposed in the form of plate tectonics to explain the phenomenon. That mountain ranges, let alone continents, are moving seems almost as unbelievable as the statement that the Earth is alive. But what is now proved, as William Blake put it, was once only imagined.

The continental drift story is instructive to think about as we contemplate the possible general acceptance of the concept of Gaian regulation and a physiology of the Earth's surface. The absence of predictive scientific models explaining generally or precisely *how* the biosphere regulates itself should not be used as evidence that the phenomenon of global bioregu-

---

* According to recent suggestions, however, there may be incipient plate tectonics on Venus; since Venus presumably has no limestone, oceans, or microbes, if plate tectonics are in fact discovered there, the proposal that life plays a key role in tectonic processes on Earth would lose much of its force.

lation does not exist. In other words, just because something happens that we don't understand does not mean that it did not happen. From the traditional theory of natural selection, which posits that evolution depends upon competition among units, a global being seems impossible: with what did it compete? What living planets fell by the wayside, allowing the selection of a highly regulated global entity? That these questions are not easily answerable suggests either a difficulty with evolutionary theory or a problem with the evidence for global regulation. Life seems to stabilize chemical compositions of its atmosphere and oceans; it seems to regulate pH (acidity), temperature, and other parameters on a global scale. If the fossil and other evidence for planetary stabilization is correct, then perhaps there is something wrong with an evolutionary theory that not only separates life into discrete units (individuals) for the sake of analysis but continues to believe that that's what they are. Perhaps life is more like a wave than a bunch of particles.

On the one hand, there are those who maintain that the phenomena explained by the concept of a Gaian Earth are better explained without invoking the idea that life chemically regulates its environment. Purveyors of these more traditional hypotheses hold that it is simpler, hence more scientific to invoke strictly chemical explanations. It is not strategic to gainsay them; they may be "right," at least within the prevailing climate of thought. On the other hand, the elegance with which disparate phenomena come together under the single explanatory umbrella of a living Earth is remarkable. Indeed, it may well be that the regulation of worldwide temperature, alkalinity, atmosphere composition, and the salinity of the oceans are only part of a more encompassing planetary physiology. Could there be, for example, such a thing as planetary psychology? I must confess that I find appealing the notion of a terrestrial intelligence encompassing, but superior to, that of humanity. Although such notions bridle most positivistic scientists, ever-wary of accusations of mysticism, we must recall that, however unconscious, the mammal body—the underlying heart-beating, temperature-modulating, pheromone-detecting physiology of all of us—is in many ways far smarter and more dependable than the human mind. An organism as old as Gaia is may have a very well-developed unconscious physiological intelligence, an intelligence of the body. And this bodily intelligence would exist on a scale thousands of miles across.

Keeping this view of a "geophysiological" rather than human intelligence in mind, we might wonder whether various forms of unusual communication (sometimes interpreted as "extrasensory perception") come about through biospheric channels, by unions too subtle to detect except insofar as they catch us by surprise. In principle, the atmosphere affords a biochemical conduit with complex molecules detectable by many organisms. Could there be molecular messages sent or hanging in the air? So, too, the experience of meaningful coincidence that Carl Gustav Jung named "synchronicity" may be due (assuming it exists) not to things metaphysical but to the functional operations of the Earth as an organism: dwelling inside a living organization that dwarfs our own in both size and complexity, what seem like suspiciously coincidental encounters may in fact be orchestrated, unknown to us, by the global superorganism. As author Peter Russell points out in *The Global Brain*, a sensitive cell in our body would no doubt often be startled by the peculiarly appropriate and repetitious order of its nurturing surroundings.[8] Never having gleaned, due to its tiny relative size, its role within a functioning animal body, the hypothetical perceiving cell would be in an almost perpetual state of wonder. Are we the thinking cells of the biosphere? Historically, in the West, the nurturance of the Earth has been considered a concession by God to his favorite creature, man. Evolutionarily, provisioning for our life is explained under the rubric of adaptationism: our ancestors were adapted to similar environments in the past. If the Earth is alive, however, we are surrounded not only by beings but by a Being.

As Lewis Thomas wrote in commemoration of the twentieth anniversary of the moon landing:

> But the moment that really mattered came later, after the equipment had been set up for taking pictures afield. There, before our eyes, causing a quick drawing in of breath the instant it appeared on television screens everywhere, was that photograph of Earth . . . it was the loveliest object human beings had ever looked upon: home.
>
> Moreover, as anyone could plainly see in the photograph, it was alive. That astonishing round thing, hanging there all alone, totally unlike any of the numberless, glistening but dead-white works of geometry elsewhere in space, was a living thing, a being . . . exploding with meaning. . . . It maintains in precision the salinity and acid-base balance of its oceans, holds constant over millions of years the exactly equilibrated components of its atmosphere with the levels of

oxygen and carbon dioxide at just the optimal levels for respiration and photosynthesis. It lives off the sun, taking in the energy it requires for its life and reflecting away the rest into the unfillable sink of space. . . . The one biological function the Earth does not yet perform to qualify for the formal definition of an organism is reproduction. But wait around, and keep an eye on it. In real life, this may turn out to be what it started to do 20 years ago. . . . the Earth may be entering the first stages of replication, scattering seeds of itself, perhaps in the form of microorganisms similar to those dominating the planet's own first life for the first two billion years of its Precambrian period. . . . Finally, as something to think about, there is the strangest of all paradoxes: the notion that an organism so immense and complex, with so many interconnected and communicating central nervous systems at work, from crickets and fireflies to philosophers, should be itself mindless. I cannot believe it.[9]

CHAPTER 8

~

The Living Earth: Hypothesis or World View?

A strong case can be made for the claim that physics has advanced into territory so boggling and shaky that the rest of science, and even physicists themselves, in their private world views, are afraid to follow. For relativity theory and, hard on its heels, quantum mechanics announce nothing less than the decline of the mechanistic world view. This world view is so deeply planted in the minds of Westerners, including scientists, that it is virtually impossible to uproot it without the soil of sanity coming loose, too. The decline of the mechanistic world view does not imply, however, that we should leap in with an organic world view to replace it, although this might seem an attractive option. In fact, taking a cue from physics itself, we might well wonder if such things can even be decided in principle. Dichotomies such as mechanism vs. organism, though interesting, may lure us into believing that reality is either one or the other, when, in fact, the universe may be neither—or both.

The properties of a global being emerge from cells rampantly growing in their environment and evolving along with that environment. Cells themselves emerge from the physical properties of molecules and atoms. The entities of particle physics are really no less, and perhaps much more, surprising than the idea of a biosphere that is "pregnant," on the verge of reproduction. In physics, the position and momentum of an electron can never, as a matter of principle and a conspiracy of nature, be simultaneously observed. This is Werner Heisenberg's uncertainty principle, which became part of Niels Bohr's more general statement of "complementarity." We cannot say whether light is "really" a particle or a wave. Experiments help create the observations they observe; there is no "outside" the universe, and thus true objectivity remains an illusion. Such a Zen universe is not lovingly embraced by a scientific community hooked on positivism, empiricism, and the hope that reality can somehow ultimately be reduced to the knowable and thus mastered. Nature may not tolerate final principles. No one can blame scientists for not wanting to speculate or interpret the meaning of nature's irresoluteness. The scientist majority has yet to come to grips with the implications of quantum physics—the magical behavior of the very small—or with the implications of modern biology—the living behavior of the Earth as a being.

What does it mean not only to say but to take seriously the statement "the Earth is *alive*"? If the air above our heads is produced and maintained by life, if a single handful of the soil on which we stand contains countless millions of gas-exchanging bacteria, fungi, and tiny animals, we are never alone. The implications of a Gaian view of the Earth extend beyond the circumscribed realm of objective science. The atmosphere breathes messages that we may or may not intercept. Sophisticated but unconscious, like the beating of our heart, the biospheric environment is autonomic —performing highly complex cycling and interspecies physiological functions without our paying the least attention to such processes. It is only —as when one drinks too much coffee and feels the heart beats fast, or has an accident and feels pain—when the system is *disturbed* that we notice it. Within the development of the biosphere it may be the disturbance generated by humanity on a global scale that brings us to the realization that the biosphere is reactive and participatory—though so effortless in its operations that usually it can be taken for granted and ignored.

All the Planet's a Stage

As mentioned, Lovelock calls his hypothesis of global biotic control "Gaia." A rare scientist who works in the main outside academia, Lovelock invented the electron capture device, still the most sensitive means of detecting tiny amounts of fluorocarbons and other gases in the atmosphere.

Much of his work has been done at his laboratory, attached to a cottage home replete with pet peacocks in the English countryside. In the late 1960s and early 1970s Lovelock's neighbor in Wiltshire was novelist William Golding. Golding was sympathetic to Lovelock's perceptions of a globally controlling life system, or cybernetic organism, that transcended plants and animals. As a name he suggested Gaia, after the Greek goddess of the Earth. A powerful theory needs a powerful name. Gaia, in its most provocative formulation, says that the Earth is an organism. Does such a perspective lend itself to verification? Is the view that the Earth is alive even testable at all?

Probably not. In March 1988, a conference was convened by the American Geophysical Union in San Diego, California. The avowed purpose of the meeting was to test Gaia's legitimacy as a scientific hypothesis. The philosophers stole the show when, in a session on epistemology, they highlighted the radical nature of this hypothesis in the modern world. For James W. Kirchner, at the University of California, Berkeley, the weak version of the hypothesis, that life alters its environment dramatically, is true enough but nothing new, while the idea that the Earth is an organism, the strong version, is not a testable hypothesis at all. The Gaia hypothesis is, Kirchner said, like saying "All the world's a stage." How can you test Shakespeare's metaphor? You can't any more than you can test Lovelock's. Kirchner said that if Shakespeare had written something like "There are footlights at the edge of the world," his statement could be tested. He could walk out and see if there were footlights. It would not be a metaphor but a research hypothesis, which is to say a hypothesis that could be shown to be false.

What is philosophically in question here is whether there exists a rigid separation between metaphor and hypothesis. On the one hand, "positivists" hold that there is an absolute, rigid distinction between hypotheses (possibilities that may or may not be "really" true) and metaphors (mere figures of speech, which, while poetic, can never be proven true because they remain analogies). On the other hand, "perspectivists" hold that with sufficient will you can create your own reality; for them, no such rigid distinction applies. We can amass evidence, but can enough ever be amassed to finally verify a theory? And does not the hypothesis itself indicate what sorts of evidence we will accept in support of it?

In reality, a rigid separation of hypothesis and metaphor is not possible. On the one hand, Gaia thinking is far more sophisticated than macrobiotics, crystal healing, and other therapeutic "new-age" fads that do not, even in principle, allow aspects of themselves to be tested and proven wrong. On the other hand, the Gaia hypothesis is not testable in any absolutely rigorous or final way. But, then, neither are the conclusions of modern physics and astronomy: the history of science has clearly shown, again and again, that today's final truths are discarded to make room for tomorrow's reality. Gaia, like quantum mechanics or molecular biology, should not only be based on propositional truth and falsity but also be always mediated by language.

It therefore matters little whether someone publishes a statement saying Gaia has been proven true or, conversely, untrue. As Oscar Wilde said, "Even things that are true can be proved." Someday Gaia theory, or some differently named version of the doctrine of "geophysiology," may be so widespread that proving or disproving it will not even enter scientists' minds as it will be ingrained in a language whose wondering will have long since turned to other things. Historian Thomas Kuhn and his less well-known predecessor Ludwik Fleck have convincingly demonstrated that analogies and metaphors are the stock and trade of science, though it takes an extremely powerful "paradigm" to replace the prevailing metaphors or metaphorical systems.[1] Nonetheless, powerful new analogies from time to time arrive that are capable of supplanting an entire old system. Johann Wolfgang von Goethe, who long dreamed of a poetic science, compared scientific theories to buildings that eventually collapse and must be abandoned. In The Possible and the Actual, which Michel Foucault has called "The most remarkable history of biology that has ever been written," French Nobel laureate François Jacob quotes biologist Jean Rostand: "Theories pass. The Frog remains."[2]

In my "metascientific" opinion, Lovelock's geophysiology—although like all other scientific theories, a system of analogies—has the proper balance of novelty and phraseology to prevail as a respectable scientific paradigm. To be taken seriously as science a theory requires that the metaphoric bases of a system of thought are not themselves continually open to question. The "geophysiological" likening of the animal body to the biosphere is part of a long tradition of microcosm-macrocosm theories in Western philosophy, and it may someday become so commonplace that its metaphorical bases are rarely questioned.

For the sake of argument, let us accept that there is a dramatic separation between Gaia as a hypothesis and Gaia as a metaphor, and that

Gaia as a hypothesis to be proven true must allow itself to be proven false. From this perspective, we might state that Gaia to be proven an organism must show evidence of reproduction. Obviously, if we consider "artificial" biospheres evidence of biospheric reproduction, then certainly the idea that the Earth is alive is a proposition that not only can be tested but also must be answered in the affirmative. If the biosphere has baby biospheres, how shall we consider it if not alive? Of course, the interpretation of self-enclosed ecosystems as "baby biospheres" need not be accepted, in which case this line of argument will not have convinced you of the biosphere's "pregnancy."

More technical lines of argument can and have been offered and accepted in support of Gaia's status as a bona-fide scientific hypothesis. In Lovelock's view, were it not for Gaia's rock-solid status as a scientific hypothesis, which results in predictions that can be tested experimentally, none of the important trace gases dimethyl sulfide, carbon disulfide, methyl iodide and chloride would have been sought and found when they were. This is still a bit different from stating that the view of Earth as organism is itself open to experimental proof. Lovelock is saying, rather, that such a view has stimulated geophysiological thinking, including the postulation of specific mechanisms that can be tested or set up as a model.

There is poetic justice in giving a *scientific* theory a name taken from Greek mythology, since science in the main has, I think, forgotten its mythological origins and nonscientific, metaphysical assumptions. It seems clear that the Gaia hypothesis, properly speaking, is not a hypothesis at all but a world view. And a nonmechanical world view cannot be legitimately debated at a scientific meeting in a culture whose mechanical world view—ultimately, particles acted upon by forces—is not open to negotiation. Thus what happened at the American Geophysical Union meeting is that an old but supremely helpful (and scientifically exciting) world view was smuggled into a world-class scientific meeting. Gaia may not, in the end, be provable as an hypothesis. It is far more than that. It is, as Karl Popper said of Darwinian evolution itself, a "metaphysical research program." Once the academics accepted the Trojan horse of a world view disguised, dressed up as a hypothesis, it was too late: a view alien to the prevailing mechanistic one had been let in; the doors were closed; the meeting began.

As the consciousness of society shifts away from the view that the universe is merely a collection of particles operated upon by outside laws, new vocabularies appear. Although Gaia bears strong traces of the "primitive" animistic belief systems of "oral" cultures, Lovelock and the scientists currently studying geophysiology in a respectable academic way are still searching for "mechanisms." Plugging into the language of cybernetics, they are looking for feedback loops and for the presence of sensitive natural "switches" that can "turn on" to release gases in short supply and "turn off" when the requisite atmospheric quantity of those gases has been sensed. They want to know how the global mean surface temperature of the Earth has stabilized and how water has avoided freezing over or boiling despite a 30 percent estimated output in the luminosity of the sun. This search for global thermostats and devices, for a description of the control processes operating computerlike at the surface of the Earth, may not be the best lexicon for speaking of the Earth. The language of cybernetics—of mechanism—should be tested with the language of geophysiology—of organism.

Destroying Science?

There was the usual discord at another Gaia conference between the scientific establishment and what climatologist Stephen Schneider has called the "ecofreaks." As the label suggests, these are people concerned with nature in a highly emotional way, a way that sometimes seems to spill over into political fanaticism. The involved political concerns of these "ecofreaks," however, may be a welcome departure from the supercilious posture of scientists who not only assume their opinions are unassailable, but—as a matter of complete and utter scientific faith— take it for granted that they are being detached and objective.

The conference was held in October 1987 in the beautiful Cornish countryside of Camelford, at a place called Worthyvale Manor. The title of the conference was "Gaia: Theory, Practice, and Implications." Amid the serenity of the damp green surroundings, the talk was ecology and philosophy, science and politics. Trying to bridge the gap between the traditional scientists and the political greens, philosopher David Abram began his talk by manipulating a green billiard ball, making it change colors to red (representing a radioactive Earth) and back again as he spoke in verse upon the topic of ecology. He had, he said, attended a talk at the State University of New York at Stony Brook by eminent evolutionary

biologist Stephen Jay Gould. At the end of the talk, Gould took a question
from the back of the room. "Could you please," a tentative voice asked,
"could you please comment on the Gaia hypothesis?"

"I'm glad you asked that," said Gould. And he continued:

> After each of the last five lectures that I have given at universities, at
> least one person has asked a question about the Gaia hypothesis. Yet
> nothing that I said in those lectures had anything to do with the Gaia
> hypothesis! This is very interesting. People are obviously very curious
> about the Gaia hypothesis. Yet I myself can't see anything in it that
> I didn't learn in grade school. Obviously the atmosphere interacts
> with life; its oxygen content, for instance, is clearly dependent on
> living organisms. But we've known this for a long time. The Gaia
> hypothesis says nothing new, it offers no new mechanisms. It just
> changes the metaphor. But metaphor is not mechanism!

Abram dramatically looked up at his audience. "Well," he said. "What
Gould failed to say is that *mechanism* itself is nothing more than a *metaphor.*

Abram did not confront Gould's question by supplying any Gaian
mechanisms because to do so would have been to use the language of
the mechanical world view in question. Indeed, criticism was leveled
that Abram is basically unscientific, even (horror of subjective horrors)
"touchy-feely" in his outlook; that there is no room for the so-called
strong version of Gaia in a scientific view of the biosphere. Kirchner, at
the AGU conference in San Diego, said, "I only came here to destroy
Gaia; Abram came here to destroy *science.*"

Return of the Pendulum

Biology may be fast approaching the uncertain ground of contemporary
physics (and perspectivist philosophy), where we realize that things are
not as certain as they seem and that *how* we look dramatically influences
what we see. Moreover, from the standpoint of the sociology of science,
it is not uncommon for a phenomenon to be noticed, yet dismissed as
unimportant by scientists until a suitable mechanism has been developed
to explain the phenomenon's occurrence. This happened with continental

drift, which was discarded as poppycock because forces to move mountains laterally were hotly debated and forces to move continents were unknown. Only after the theory of plate tectonics was developed to explain paleo-magnetic reversals on the ocean floor, as well as the linear distribution of earthquakes and volcanoes, was evidence for the movement of conti-nents entirely accepted. Paradoxically, as mechanisms for Gaian inter-action accumulate, it may come to be accepted scientifically and undermine the language of mechanism itself.

In my view, the historical pendulum has already begun to swing back again, toward the ancient view that the world, like the individual, is a sensitive, live, unpredictable entity—an organism.

Abram proposed that in its development, science had to compromise with institutionalized religion. To do so, it was necessary to keep the metaphor of mechanism alive simply for scientists to pursue their own studies. Why? Because a mechanism implies a *creator* and reinforces the traditional idea of a God outside the world. That many working scientists are atheists does not mean that they are not heir to a world view with many important theological roots.

The Newtonian universe was seen as the perfect mechanism, clock-work designed by a master artificer. Science evolved from the idea of a constantly intervening, "hands-on" God to God the inventor, able to create the cosmos and leave it to run its own course. Before Charles Darwin, London encyclopedia publisher Robert Chambers anonymously advanced the idea in his 1844 *Vestiges of the Natural History of Creation* that God did not separately create species and actively oversee them, but created life on Earth only once, in the beginning, and had let it run its vital course. God was like the creator of a fine Swiss watch. As science progresses further, it begins to ponder the origin and fate of the cosmos itself, leaving little room for God conceived of as outside creation. The mechanism comes to be seen as self-organizing.

Note that a mechanism that makes itself is really not a mechanism at all, but a kind of organism. Even in Charles Darwin's term, "natural selection"—which presented organized religion with its most reeling blow yet from the hands of science—we see homage paid, albeit tacitly, to the idea of mechanism: "natural selection" (coined in opposition to "artificial selection," or the breeding of other species such as pigeons and dogs by human beings) implies an artificer—a selector performing his actions from the outside. According to Abram, the pervasiveness of the mechanistic metaphor derives from its usefulness in keeping peace with those afraid that science will destroy the idea of God altogether. Who needs God if creation is self-creating? From a philosophical standpoint, God moves from being transcendent, outside the world, to becoming immanent, within the world.

From the distant or punitive father God we move to a female deity bathing us in her presence. Gaia is not only a goddess, she is immanent. We are of and in her body. People seem thirsty not only for a female as opposed to a male deity but also for immanence rather than transcendence. Some anthropologists believe prehistoric peoples worshiped the moon and female fertility goddesses. If this is so, then the rise of Gaian "religion" —a world feeling for planetary unity and interconnectedness—may represent a turn back to a sociocultural myth of Earth, the likes of which we haven't seen in thousands of years. An understanding of the Earth will require new techniques of unconscious resonance, new means of speaking. According to Abram, French philosopher Merleau-Ponty was in the midst of wrestling with such problems when he died.

> It seems clear that as long as humanity continues to use language strictly for its own ends, as if it belonged to our species alone, then we will find ourselves estranged from our actions. If as Merleau's work indicates it is not merely *this* body but the whole visible, sensual world that is the deep flesh of language, then surely our very words will continue to tie our selves, our families, and our nations into knots until we free our voice to return to the real world that supports it—until we allow it to respond to the voice of the threatened rainforests, the whales, the rivers, the birds, and indeed to speak for the living, untamed Earth which is its home. . . . The real Logos, after Merleau-Ponty, is Eco-Logos. . . . Unlike the language of information processing and cybernetics, Merleau-Ponty's descriptive phenomenology provides a way to think and to disclose the living fields of interaction from our experienced place *within* them.[3]

Merleau-Ponty stressed a "perceptual logic" reigning underneath all our categories. The *"sensible world,"* wrote Merleau-Ponty, "is this perceptual logic . . . and this logic is neither produced by our psychophysical constitution, nor produced by our categorical equipment, but lifted from a *world* whose inner framework our categories, our constitution, our 'subjectivity' render explicit. . . ."[4] A deep language of Earth would not necessarily resemble the language of cybernetics, with its emphases on the communication and control of animals and machines.

Such a language would not shrink from its source but would drink from it thirstily, acknowledging the play of its "eco-logic" origins. If language is, as Martin Heidegger says, the "house of being," so the material Earth is the house of our bodies. Many so-called primitive cultures believe that animals are messages from a deity or the assumption by an unseen deity of a visible form. If we recall that all language is in and of the Earth, we will come to the startling conclusion that language is not ultimately or solely a human thing. The destiny of language is far greater than all we know by the name of "human."

Picasso's Eye

The history of science reveals that there are no absolute truths. The late Robert Garrels, a Harvard University professor who spent his last years in the Department of Marine Science at the University of South Florida, is internationally recognized as one of the two or three foremost experts on global geochemistry. Yet Garrels himself quipped, "We all build more and more complicated geochemical models until no one understands anyone else's model. The only thing we do know is that our own is wrong." And: "The chief purpose of models is not to be right or wrong but to give us a place to store our data."[5]

We all perceptually simplify, creating views of the world as complete as they are inaccurate. It is said that a man once confronted Picasso and complained about the artist's abstractions of the female figure—all those chunky Catalonians with extra eyes and misplaced limbs. Picasso maintained that his paintings were quite realistic. Every painting, Picasso said, no matter how strange, is a version of the truth. But reaching into his pocket, the man withdrew a photograph. It was a snapshot of his wife. He showed it to Picasso and asked:

"Can't you paint realistically—like that?"

"Is that really what she looks like?"

"Yes," said the man.

"She must be very flat then," said Picasso, "and quite small."

There is perhaps no representation of the Earth more inadequate than the world view that sees mankind as the chosen species, above nature, and so technologically potent that we can control the biosphere that we inhabit.

Your Majesty, Humanity

The Picasso story graphically illustrates that our ideas of reality may be absurd in the extreme. We would do well to assume Picasso's radical scrutiny as we contemplate the nature of our role as human beings in planet Earth. It is common to believe that human beings, if not the pinnacle of creation, are the highest example of evolution, the most evolved animal; but is it not curious that this flattering judgment about the supreme status of humans in the biosphere has been decided by the very species doing the judging?

Freud compared the ego to a circus clown parading about. The clown pretends with simple gestures to have caused the effects that he is only miming.[6] For example, a flying trapeze artist might do a triple somersault in the air: the ego-clown would make circling motions with his fingers, bowing as the acrobat caught his swing. So, too, as a species, our control over the biota, the sum of organisms interacting at the Earth's surface, may be illusory. Our history is marked by wars and weapons, ever more technologically sophisticated and destructive than before. It is also marked by creating new technologies such as agriculture and industry to overcome former limits of the environment. Continuing at current rates of population growth, in only a few centuries the human biomass, the sheer weight of new human flesh, would expand off the Earth into space at a velocity faster than that of light; obviously that is impossible and so our growth as a species must dramatically decline in accord with earthly resources. In our self-centered way we pretend to be kings of the biosphere—stewards and engineers in charge of the environment and other species. However, if the Earth has a true physiology, our growth will be circumscribed and our role limited.

The means nature has invented for reproduction continually exceed one's expectations. They are not limited to the simple copying of bacteria but extend to the more complex asexual dance of mitosis. In plants, fungi, protoctists, and animals, reproduction is often still more elaborate, entailing a meeting of the sexes and the cellular permutation of mitosis known as meiosis. But it would be short-sighted to think reproductive complexity reaches its height with the sexually reproducing animal. Reproduction also includes situations in which members of other species are integrally involved, such as the dependence of some flowering plants upon certain birds, insects, or bats. Many plant reproductive acts depend for their fertilization upon the eating behaviors of animals. These famous reproductive acts (the birds and the bees) show that nature does not always use like to create like, but may depend upon the mediation of totally unlike individuals. In the same manner as a given flower depends upon a bee for its propagation, so the terrestrial biosphere, in begetting technological miniatures of itself, requires human mediation to complete this, its first reproductive cycle.

The reproductive metamorphosis of planet Earth is more like the complex, associative, mediated reproduction exemplified by the birds and the bees than it is like the immediate reproduction of amoebae or the sexual reproduction of people. If the biosphere uses humanity to produce technology to reproduce itself, then biospheric reproduction would appear more complex, though no less an example of reproduction, than other reproductive acts in nature. It sounds teleological to say that the biosphere uses humanity to create technology to reproduce herself, but it may be no more teleological to say so than to claim that the human body produces sweat in order to cool itself. In both cases, we need not be discussing a thinking, humanlike entity, but only the unconscious purposiveness of an "autonomic nervous system." It is not us but the geophysiology of the Earth that may be "in charge."

If this whole, spooky, science-fiction scenario of the biosphere using us to accomplish its own ends is true, why would we be privy to the bubbling up of ecological consciousness? In other words, the spawning of technology, a prerequisite to extraterrestrial expansion of the biosphere via its "offspring," has been aided by human greed, egocentricity, and isolation. But this may no longer be the case. It may be that the time has come, from a biospheric vantage point, for us to glimpse a new role for ourselves; no longer isolationists, selfishly rearing technology for our own ends, but integrationists—connectors and vectors of disparate parts of the biosphere—no longer murderers but intermediaries and matchmakers among the millions of species participating in the life of the biosphere. In such an altered outlook, technology, language, and science would be seen to belong not to the ephemeral species of humans, incubated by the biosphere, but to the lasting destiny of our pregnant Mother: Earth.

FIRE

Don't you see, that which was seed will get green herb and herb will turn into ear and ear into bread. Bread will turn into nutrient liquid, which produces blood, from blood semen, embryo, men, corpse, Earth, rock and mineral and thus matter will change its form ever and ever and is capable of taking any natural form.
—Giordano Bruno

It is said by some with whom I have conversed upon this subject, that the machines can never be developed into animate or quasi-animate existences, inasmuch as they have no reproductive system, nor seem ever likely to possess one. If this be taken to mean that they cannot marry, and that we are never likely to see a fertile union between two vapour-engines with the young ones playing about the door of the shed . . . I will readily grant it. But the objection is not a very profound one. No one expects that all the features of the now existing organisations will be absolutely repeated in an entirely new class of life. The reproductive system of animals differs widely from that of plants, but both are reproductive systems. Has nature exhausted her phases of this power? . . . What is a reproductive system, if it be not a system for reproduction?
—Samuel Butler

CHAPTER 9

~

Titans

We like to think of ourselves as the children of Mother Earth. For example, Homer praised Gaia as "Mother of everything . . . of all gods, and wife of the starry Uranus!" and wrote to her that "children of humans originate from you and so does the luscious fruit." But if you look up Gaea in a book of Greek mythology you find that the children of mother Earth were monsters and not humans. These were the Titans, a family of giants. In a similar manner, the offspring of the biosphere will be gigantic, dwarfing our notion of what is human even as it extends that notion into new realms. Someday atmospheres like ours may emerge over planets and the moons such as Titan and Triton presently uninhabitable within our solar system. The dissemination of the biosphere will depend on the descendants of those "monsters" we presently know as machines.

Andromeda Strain

In Michael Crichton's novel *The Andromeda Strain*, a deadly extraterrestrial germ falls to Earth and begins killing humans and laboratory monkeys with such speed that quarantine and nuclear explosion of the infectious agent is considered an appropriate way to ensure the safety of the U.S. population. An interesting anomaly of the otherworldly pest is that, unlike all known terrestrial life forms, it has no amino acids.

This science-fiction story set in the future is not nearly as strange as the analogous, if unrecognized, real-life situation of the present. Perhaps it is no coincidence that machines, a rapidly spreading form of matter that are often destructive to life, also lack amino acids, the components of proteins found in all known organisms. Although part of us, and lifelike in their organization, machines are built largely of non-proteinaceous materials similar to the hard parts of living organisms.

Part of life's problems with the technologies humans have sired is that new chemical compounds have become introduced into the planetary environment—chemical compounds for which there are, as yet, few or no means of decomposition into the biospheric circulation. If industrial by-products and technological toxins could be broken down by bacteria and fungi into constituents usable by life, then technology would seem less unnatural. To a degree, this absorption into the global ecosystem is already underway: bacteria are able to metabolize some refractory materials we have dumped into the environment such as naphthalene; fungi, termites, and bacteria rot through the tough cellulose of forests, thereby continually forestalling the "natural" pollution crisis that began long before the origins of man. In the short term, however, pollutants pile up in the Earth. This is dangerous especially to us because it puts into circulation poisons for which there are currently no biospheric antidotes and we begin to smother in nonbiodegradable throwaways. In the long run, undoubtedly organisms will evolve means of digesting technological excess. The rise of cities, of automobiles and asphalt, and the disruption of the planetary ecosystem could be seen by future historians as a natural phenomenon. Neobiologists might construe present ecological problems as part of an all-natural if painful process of planetary development, the growing pains of a terraqueous being.

Technology starts as an "Andromeda strain" opposed to and generally threatening the rest of nature. But then technology moves through humanity to become infused into the infrastructure of life on Earth. Because we use it so much, and because we are so widespread, technology transforms, weaving into the totality of life's texture and tenure on Earth. It then remakes that entire texture from which it derives. Soviet biologist D. V. Panfilov suggests that the living matter of the biosphere assumes two forms: a reproducing form and a nonreproducing, or "somatic," form whose purpose it is to help move the reproducing form. Somatic matter (from the legs of gazelles to whirling maple seeds) is an effective transport mechanism for the spread of reproducing genes. But, as with the proportion of mass of DNA to the cell around it, the proportion of reproductive matter to somatic matter in the biosphere is very small: life's most intriguing phenomena are found not in the realm of genes but at a genetic remove, in patterns of somatic matter—the hard body parts built around the reproducing genes—whose purpose it is to safeguard and transport them. Adhering to Panfilov's distinction, technology may be seen as a form of somatic living matter—part of the system that encases and deploys the reproducing genes. It is an unwieldy and stiff part of a growing planetary body that already is rich in compounds (including metals and their derivatives) such as chalk, fluorite, and magnetite.

Fractals and Fusing

Life on Earth as a whole is coming together; it is focusing, fusing. The biosphere is older and more rugged, complex, and elastic than any species or community. The biosphere is not, as Plato considered astral bodies, simply animal or zoological in nature, though the biosphere does live and breathe. (Although the concentration of atmospheric carbon dioxide is rising—annual hemispheric peaks in carbon dioxide level of the atmosphere are measured weekly at Mauna Loa, Hawaii—measurements clearly show a breathlike rising and falling in time to the seasonal spread of vegetation.) At least superficially, the level of organic integration within the biosphere seems more loosely knit and closer to that of a colonial alga or a seaweed than to that of, say, a dandelion or a dog. For example, myxamoebae feed independently on bacteria, but when they become too crowded and run out of food, they release a chemical compound called acrasin. Under the influence of this chemical, they coalesce into a creeping chunk of slime known as a slug. In the species *Dictyostelium* the slug forms a hard stalk with a cap at the top full of spores that, when released, regenerate back into individual swimming amoebae. The members of other species of slime mold slide over wet logs. Spores mailed to laboratories and stashed away have been known to regenerate under humid conditions. On logs the slippery mass dries, forming brittle, sometimes brightly colored structures—spore towers that look like tiny, rounded coral or yellow mushrooms. These towers give off a puff of dust if touched; the spores are generally disseminated by a gust of wind. In some species, the spores do not immediately grow into spore towers but return to a free-living state as independent amoebae. These have a kind of orgy, from which is conceived the fan-shaped feeding mass that crawls over logs and laboratory benches, leaving a track of slime. (If forced through a cotton seive at this stage, the slime mold will recognize and reconstitute itself on the other side.) If such apparently independent amoebae on the forest floor can coalesce into an organized mass, of what might the biosphere as a whole be capable?

A "fractal" is an irregular-appearing geometric figure, which, upon closer examination, exhibits self-similarity: that is, it enfolds its entire pattern into each tiny fragment. The overall fractal repeats itself in itself at various scales of analysis: the (w)hole fractal is in the hole of the whole. Although an exploration of the properties and usefulness of fractals has evolved only recently in mathematics, being made possible by the introduction of high-speed computers and graphics programs, the idea of the fractal, of a part that contains the whole, is probably as old as civilization. Tendai, a sect of Japanese Buddhism, teaches that the whole and its parts meld with each other—that the entire cosmos exists within a sand grain or a hair. Is the structure of the biosphere itself not in some sense "fractal"? Is it a matter of biological identity—of organization as organism—cropping up at progressively more inclusive levels, from cell, to animal, to technological biospheres—themselves global replicas, planetary ecosystems in miniature? Sophisticated fractal graphics—patterns that repeat their overall structure in their minutest parts—became possible only with the aid of the modern high-speed computer, able to perform the same operation many times to generate intriguing, detailed designs. I suspect that the reproduction of the biosphere similarly emerges from a simple operation performed a great many times. This relatively simple operation is the replication of organisms within the crowded environment they are continually altering.

Individuality

In our discussion of the camel as a community and the Earth as an organism, we have confronted the limits of individuality from two sides. In general, the microscopic view of "organism as society" (as in the camel) is more difficult to attain, more abstract than its macroscopic reverse, "society as organism." You may lift the plastic shade of a commercial airliner and stare down at what looks very nearly like part of a giant body in action. Minute lines of colored cars stream in and out of streets like the watery insides of an amoeba or like ants marching in file. Technology gives us the opportunity not only to rise above the system of which we are a part but also to take time-lapse photography and condense time periods. And yet the body itself is a kind of society, a cellular superorganism that has been finely honed by billions of years of natural selection.

Just as thirst and hunger are a response of the cells in our body to incipient shortages of food and water, so the agitation of individuals in a population, sometimes rising to the scale of social turmoil, is an advance warning of resource shortages. The human body is a much more integrated population than a city. When thirsty, we look to sate ourselves with drink. Society as a whole behaves comparably when television focuses our attention on water shortages in Los Angeles, domestic child abuse cases, Ethiopian famine, civil unrest, and so on. These are not pleasant topics, but neither is thirst a pleasant sensation. Environmental limits constrain both the social organism and the organismic society. In both cases, we either must find the resources adequate to maintain a healthy population or we must limit the growth of that population.

Because they have been taught that natural selection works at the level of the individual, it may be thought that natural mechanisms cannot exist to control the growth of populations. But "individual" plants and animals are really "populations" of cells—genetically, former organisms—acting in concert. Although we cannot pinpoint the exact mechanisms for regulating birth and dealing out death, both these acts enhance the individuality of overcrowded populations. Nature accomplishes these ends through her own means, and they may be part of a primeval government far more effective, experienced, and, when necessary—harsher and more *devious*—than any bureaucracy set up by human beings. As Bernard Campbell puts it:

> Natural selection does not generate happiness or contentment unless it has survival value. If our survival depends on miscarriages, high infant mortality, mental deficiency, criminality, sexual perversion, and so on, they will remain with us in spite of the tremendous efforts of the medical professions. But there is an alternative to hand: cultural methods of population control have been known for thou-

sands of years, and though infanticide and even abortion may seem cruel, they are surely better than the biological responses to over-population.[1]

We are beyond mere imagery here. It is not simply an analogy to point out that human populations behave as if they were on their way to becoming organisms, organisms whose constituent "cells"—in this case, individual persons—must have their propensity to reproduce strictly regulated if the populations they are part of are to achieve ordered specialization and, thus, success in relation to other such (increasingly organized) populations. As the importance to all of us of friends, lovers, family, and society attests, we are not mere individuals but networks, integrated with technology and other species into urban and other aggregates. We care what our neighbors think because our neighbors act and react, and our livelihoods and lives stand to suffer if we veer too far from the unwritten collective guidelines over which none of us as individuals has much control. Society and governments appear to be run by human beings; in fact, society and governments may represent more organic patterns of reproduction, specialization, and crowd control—patterns whose general shape is to be found in any number of species. It may be an ecological fact that crowded organisms *become* superorganisms acting at new, higher levels of organization. Scientists who dispute this must ignore the biochemical, physical, and economic ties that bind all of us—humans and other species—together and make it impossible for any of us to act alone.

So-called group selection—the notion that natural selection can preserve not only individuals, as Darwin stressed, but also societies or groups of organisms—has been out of favor for years now in evolutionary biology. Some of this disfavor may even be deserved. For example, it used to be common in biological literature (and still is in public broadcasting nature documentaries) for virtually any sort of animal behavior at all to be explained in terms of the "good of the species." But this is an abstraction; a species' members need not have any strong biochemical, spatial, or ecological attachments. Far more cohesive an entity is the community, groups of interacting populations taken in their local biogeochemical context. Camels and nations are communities, and so are you. The chain of community is made of biochemical links; a cow, for example, without its internal reserves of cellulose digesters and methanogens, would die of starvation even if surrounded by lush fields of grass. The components of communities cannot always be separated without death to many parties ensuing. Thus they evolve as units. From a community selection standpoint, some forms of seemingly stupid and risky behavior undoubtedly enhance the survival of the groups to which the self-endangering individual is bound. Although group selection has been mathematically "disproven," this only alerts us to the inadequacies of mathematics in modeling ecology and to the faulty assumptions on which many models have been based. Indeed, community selection, or something like it, must be invoked to explain the evolution of mathematicians and biologists themselves.

Selfishness

Edward O. Wilson, a neo-Darwinian entomologist at Harvard University, is a major founder of sociobiology—a wing of evolutionary biology that discusses the effects of genes on behavior, including human behavior. Wilson has elaborated the traditional view that evolution is a competitive affair of individuals struggling for selfish advantage. Although Wilson has spoken of social insect colonies (and even specialized scientists, in the aggregate) as superorganisms, he has largely accepted the view that evolution is a matter of "individuals" surviving. But, as we have seen, individuality is elusive. From the nucleated cell of the amoeba, whose mitochondria bear the genetic fingerprints of the respiring bacteria from which they evolved, to the cow and camel, all life forms are colonies and symbiotic collectives. There are no exceptions. Nonetheless, biologists insist on discussing individuals, partly for the sake of convenience, partly out of habit, and partly out of loyalty to professional trends. In addition, biologists can *feel* their own subjective individuality; the individuality of a society of animals or a community of mixed species of organisms is less immediate. Nonetheless, biologists have, in the wake of the discovery of the DNA molecule, adjusted themselves to the idea that the gene, rather than the individual animal, is the "true" unit of selection.

Using theories such as "kin selection" (developed by evolutionary biologist William D. Hamilton), Wilson has suggested that very social members of the insect order *Hymenoptera* (such as wasps, ants, and bees) form superorganisms because they are such close relatives. Members of this order share an unusual life cycle in which all sisters are genetically very similar, two times as closely related as human sisters. According to kin selection, this predisposes insects in this order to tend the queen, to share food, and to undertake other forms of altruistic behavior that seem inexplicable if evolution is simply a matter of the genetic advantages that accrue to individual members. Since some individuals in insect societies don't even reproduce themselves, and since some spend all their time tending to their relatives, Wilson, Hamilton, and other founding sociobiologists have had to move the unit of selection down from Darwin's individual animal to the genes within that animal. In this way, one can conceive that organisms safeguard their own genes by altruistically protecting them in the bodies of others. The gene need not recognize itself in this theory but merely influence the brain that recognizes genetic effects in body and behavior. Like many concepts in science, the idea that genes are the true units of natural selection is an attractive oversimplification.

Oxford evolutionist Richard Dawkins took this idea to its logical popular science extreme, proclaiming that our bodies are mere robots—vehicles programmed by the genes. Nonetheless, after developing his narrow "selfish gene" concept, even Dawkins was forced to admit that genes in the body of a member of one species may select for traits in the bodies of members of another species, even ones thousands of miles away. (This he called the "extended phenotype"—that is, the ability of an organism's genes, its genotype, to affect not only the shape and behavior of its own body, but also, by affecting in various ways intermediary organisms, the make-up and action of other organisms' bodies, technically known as "phenotypes.") Thus, as the "selfishness" concept is extended, it becomes very nebulous indeed. No gene in me can live by itself but only as part of a network or aggregate of other encased genes. Now Wilson has admitted that selection above the level of genes and individuals must be taken seriously as a theoretical possibility.[2] But to keep to a consistent neo-Darwinian view of the world, Wilson and Dawkins themselves must be regarded as the outcome of transpecies teamwork, a biochemical intermingling among cells (with and without nuclei) that can in no way be construed as a simple struggle among separate and selfish genes or individuals. The symbiotic merging of cells and genes is a prerequisite to the dogma that evolution is a matter of individual survival—whether these individuals be considered animals or genes.

In later discussions, Wilson too had to draw the selfish individual and gene idea out to its vanishing point. Perhaps to compensate for a theory accused of being simplistic, social Darwinist, ethnocentric, reductionist, and sexist—in other words, of justifying the dog-eat-dog social status quo—Wilson developed the euphonious neologism "biophilia," from the Greek words *philía* meaning love and *bíos* meaning life.[3] Biophilia is our deep attraction to life, even distantly related forms of life with which we share relatively few genes, such as snakes, woolly spiders, and preying mantises. Taking a broad perspective, this seems a necessary and convincing correction. After all, we are physiologically serenaded by the aromas of flowers and fruit; we feel serene in the presence of gardens, fish, tropical birds, and domestic animals; and we encourage the propagation of species from cattle to brewer's yeast by using products as quotidian as shoes and beer.

No organism is a biochemical island; each affects and is in turn affected by its surroundings. The growth of each changes the environment of others, with the result that individual selection is an abstraction, an ideal, and an oversimplification, no matter what entity—gene, animal, or community—one wants to attach to the label "individual." All organisms in symbiosis or biochemical partnership, all organisms cultivated or domesticated, all organisms that produce substances eaten or used by their neighbors are in some sort of community relationship. And this, of course, includes all organisms on Earth. The problem of evolutionary terminology here is illuminated by some commonplaces of Eastern philosophy. In Tao and in Buddhism—and, in the West, in the writings of Nietzsche and of quantum mechanics—the distinction between subject and object has been put to intense questioning. This distinction is critical to the problem of evolutionary terminology: the term "natural selection" suggests that there is an abstract entity, natural selection (the subject) acting upon and selecting things, namely biological units, individuals of some type (the object). The distinction may be more an artifact of linear language, of the relationship between pronouns, nouns, and verbs, than the non-thinglike reality quantum physicist David Bohm calls the "rheomode," however. Certainly genes, organisms, and groups of organisms reproduce; they do so at different but always limited rates, and they appear to do so differently depending on how you look at them. But there is no outside principle—in this case, some real entity we might associate with the noun "natural selection"—there is no *limitor* selecting them.

Why, in short, call selfish those genes that maximize the growth of completely different genes? In feeding and clothing and housing ourselves—by wearing cotton underwear and leather shoes and silk scarves—we are propagating genes other than "our own": the genes of cotton plants, cows, and silk worms. Since all these animals and plants and microbes are involved in our keeping ourselves fit, what are these selfish genes doing, if they can live only in an environment that is the product of completely different genes? It appears that the neo-Darwinian attempt to explain altruism as the result of individual selfishness has required not only the redefinition of the individual (from an animal into a gene) but also an inversion of the meaning of selfishness.

Clownfish protect themselves in the stinging tentacles of sea anemones. Giant clams eat the algae that grow protected inside their giant shells. Barracudas allow small fish to clean their razor-sharp teeth. These examples provide a technicolor backdrop to the traditional black-and-white scene of evolution being a battle in which only the most brutal survive. Perhaps it is time to shift our focus and see the colorful, symbiotic view as primary; perhaps the time has come to allow the grey spectacle of individual survival to float into the background of evolutionary thought. How can we speak honestly of selfish genes or animals when the most successful organisms on Earth are precisely those that help propagate themselves by aligning their interests and strengths with others? The problem of whether evolution is marked more by competition or cooperation resembles the question of whether lovers fall for those who are like themselves or opposite in nature. We may help others of our kind, knowing what they like and that they are like us. Or we may be attracted to opposite beings, whose strengths compensate our weaknesses, and vice versa. In evolution, a perfect match is not for life but forever; symbiotically merged beings begin to compete with their own kind, and in their own right. The two forces—competition and cooperation—are always at work in each individual. In fact, the point of their separation into opposites is itself a place of convergence.

Future individuals may possess new properties, and not resemble animals or other organisms we know. One example of such individuality is portrayed in John Varley's science-fiction yarn *Overdrawn at the Memory Bank* in which there appears a computerized planet Earth, its weather, citizens, and even Humphrey Bogart film library memories controlled by a global corporation doubling as a world government. Future organisms, biospheres, will be as different from humans and machines as a person is from bacteria.

CHAPTER 10

~

Trouble in the Body Politic

Rapidly growing populations either transform or collapse. Technology can overcome limited resources by drawing on new resources or by devising new means of extraction of food and energy. Gasohol, the use of corn waste for automobile fuel, is a potential example of such a future technology; growing corn, which allowed native Americans to settle in the great cities of Middle and South America, is an example of a past technology that permitted populations to expand by overcoming what were once limitions. The technological overcoming of environmental limits is in large part the story of human natural history. It is a natural history that is coming to a head.

The worldwide population has grown from about 1 billion people in 1600 to over 5 billion today. Some 6 to 10 billion Earthlings are expected here by the turn of the century. This striking expansion in human numbers, exceeding all Malthusian expectations, results from our increasing abilities in resource extraction—in the gathering and production of new kinds of food and energy. The world population has been periodically checked by plagues, wars, famines, and so on; but these are temporary fixes, not permanent solutions. Without voluntary or involuntary population mechanisms preventing further population growth, or new revolutions in resource extraction to keep pace with the increasing numbers, the average standard of living of people on Earth is destined to fall drastically.

Some nations, however, are showing a decline in birth rate, and institutions such as the United Nations, the World Bank, and the University of Chicago, extrapolating this trend, all project a stabilization of the world population between 8 and 12 billion by the middle of the twenty-first century.

Rats resemble humans as profligately reproducing mammals. Rats were the carrier of the bacterium that fatally visited Europe and other continents, conferring bubonic plague and helping lend the adjective "dark" to the European Middle Ages. We retain little regard for these rodents, often using them in psychological and medical research, in part, perhaps, because they remind us of ourselves. It is true that experiments with mice, rats, and guinea pigs have very limited applicability to humanity, since their anatomy and physiology differ from ours. For one thing, they are smaller and more stupid. Yet, from a generalized biospheric vantage point, the rat-human analogy is perhaps closer than we care to admit. Rats are mammals with brains, able to thrive in cities in massive numbers as they reproduce with abandon—indeed, I would venture that the ability of cockroaches, rats, and pigeons to reproduce in tandem with urban human beings, to accompany us in our reproductive profligacy, is one of the prime reasons we often find these creatures repulsive. A science-fiction writer might base a story on the information that small rodents can survive carbon monoxide concentrations far greater than can any human: where carbon monoxide destroys the ability of our red blood cells to carry oxygen, mice can survive complete saturation of their blood with carbon monoxide. Because they are so small, they can get the oxygen they need by diffusion through the lungs and skin. In this respect, they are, then, better adapted to the technical habitat of humans than we are.

Universe 133

Margaret Mead called psychologist John B. Calhoun her "favorite wild man." Calhoun has studied rodent populations at the National Institute of Mental Health.[1] There he found that mice, if they are housed and fed, will have sex and reproduce in the profligate habit to which they are accustomed. But he noticed that the mice, after transgressing optimal levels of population density in their closed laboratory setting, underwent dramatic behavior changes. In one set of experiments, Calhoun began with eight pairs of mice. He put them in an eighteen-foot-wide, four-level dwelling named "Universe 133." Calhoun looked on as the mice bloomed to nearly 1600 members in their circumscribed space; then the population crashed. The decline was accompanied by the persistence of juvenile behaviors: female mice wandered about aimlessly; males huddled together in masses. A pathological behavior known as "nipping" arose: mice turned aggressive, bit their universe-mates regularly, and exhibited the particularly cruel and tasteless behavior of grabbing weaker neighbors by their tails and swinging them about from little platforms. In general, Calhoun notes, there was a lack of drive and a sense of apathy. Attacked mice did not flee, and if they did their would-be attackers rarely pursued them.

While people are by no means rats, both are mammals, and both may have, although with significant differences, machinery built into them as individuals to compensate for too-high density at the level of populations. It is possible that the rats' streetcorner behavior, a population-level depression that almost seems a rodent version of adolescent nihilism in a nuclear age, is a response to what philosopher Peter Allport Frank calls "social-unit stress." Allport (Frank is a pseudonym) distinguishes between environmental stress and social-unit stress. Environmental stress induces organisms to band together to overcome natural dangers such as cold or predators: aggressive baboons, for instance, might overcome environmental stress by forming social units. Ironically, stress soon begins to build up in the social units designed to counter environmental stress. This is social-unit stress. Social-unit stress leads to the differentiation, migration, or reproduction of the social units—exposing them once more to conditions in which they may find themselves again subjected to environmental stress.

Can the sociopathic behavior of Calhoun's "nippers" be understood in terms of social-unit stress—overcrowding? Groups of organisms that reproduce indefinitely in closed settings or situations of limited resource availability are much more likely to suffer major population setbacks as a result of their unrestrained reproductive profligacy than are populations that somehow control themselves. About three generations after the mice reached what Calhoun considered to be their optimum population density, the population of Universe 133 completely lost interest in reproducing. Their pathological behavior, combined with a lack of sexuality, led to a precipitous collapse in the population. Ultimately, all the inhabitants of Universe 133 died.

Biologists postulate two kinds of population control: "density-dependent"

and "density-independent." A density-dependent population control occurs when a given population reaches a certain critical mass, at which
time the control "mechanism"—which may be as simple as the production
of local wastes poisonous to those who produce them—comes into play.
Biologists have speculated that such mechanisms, though they kill in the
short run, may in the long run save life by forestalling total resource
depletion. In the case of Universe 133, restraining reproduction after
optimal population density was reached apparently served little purpose.
But one might wonder whether mice lack means of controlling the growth
of their populations once they reach a certain level. For example, researchers A. S. Parkes and H. M. Bruce noticed that pregnant mice tend
to undergo spontaneous abortion if exposed even to the smell of a strange,
absent male—one that has simply rummaged about before in the cage.
This smell of another male may represent a turn toward dangerously
overcrowded conditions or it may be a sign of impending resource depletion. It is not impossible that the so-called "Bruce effect" of spontaneous
mice abortion may be one of many rodent population control mechanisms.

Calhoun trained groups of overcrowded rats to cooperate. He had
them approach water fountains in twos and use feeders only in the presence
of certain other rats, which together formed a "clan." Calhoun found that
such rats were better able to adapt to conditions of increased crowding
than was a similar, control group. By training the rodents to form social
units, Calhoun taught them to protect themselves against environmental
stress. The relative success of cooperative rats may be understood as a
reduction of environmental stress through the formation of new social
units. Is it impossible to imagine an Earth so overcrowded with rats that
they, however stupid, begin developing the rudiments of cooperative technical civilization? MIT astronomer Philip Morrison has wondered how
long it would take termites to build a radiotelescope; he concludes that,
lacking cultural evolution (that is, language, tool-using ability, and so
forth), they might do it, but it would take a very long time. Rodents are
less social than wasps, ants, bees, and termites, but then they are mammals
with brains and limbs similar to those that led to the opposable thumb.
It seems certain that rats would take far less time than Morrison's termites
to reach the nearest star.

Calhoun has applied his findings on rodents to humans and has
projected—in agreement with other studies—that between the years 2042
and 2083 the world population will reach some 9 billion. Calhoun believes

that thereafter a steep decline will occur. This steep decline corresponds to a point of "no return" between 2.5 and 4.0 generations after optimal population density is reached. Calhoun calculates that the 1975 human population was already twice its optimum. Encouraged by the initial agreement of the rodent and human situations, Calhoun extrapolates that, after a final spurt, the number of people will level off at around 2 billion in the middle of the twenty-third century. This steep decline corresponds to the dramatic decreases Calhoun witnessed in his rodent populations. It thus does not necessarily apply to us human beings who have already, and perhaps prematurely, developed high technology ranging from agriculture to biospherics—technologies of the sort that can dramatically enhance what ecologists call "carrying capacity"—in this case the ability of the biosphere to provide for human beings.

I remember my paternal grandfather apocalyptically predicting, in the Judeo-Christian tradition, that my generation would see a world crisis. It would, he said, come from the ever-growing planetary disparity between the rich and the poor. The poor nations of the south, he ventured, would pit themselves against the richer ones of the north. Perhaps his involvement in union-management struggles in this country early in this century colored his perception. Certainly a growing disparity between rich and poor could sow the seeds for major squabbles ahead. As we all know, and would often rather forget, the sickle can be pummeled into a spear and back again—making plowshares and swords draw from the same economy, ever circling in its sweetly vicious inner nature. Will a world war be required to bring humankind back into manageable parity with the planetary environment? I would rather predict, albeit more with hope than fear, that biospherics—and by this I mean open bioshelters on Earth, as well as closed structures in space—may prove to be the next great transformative technology of humanity's tenure on planet Earth. Biospherics could once again expand the realm of human dwelling and our capacity to feed ourselves, while also demonstrating that human happiness can never be dismantled from the other species upon which we depend. Biospheres, in other words, could help avert the potential for world war by expanding habitable territory, by marrying technology and ecology into forms that transcend—and thus reestablish—the very limits of human beings.

During our history as a species, growth in populations must often have reduced environmental stress. Troops of adult males hunted large mammals; in the village women helped each other look after and teach the children. These cooperative efforts allowed them to work far more effectively than if they had to do things alone. The Jews of the Old Testament were a pastoral, paternalistic, and agricultural tribe whose methods of survival became incorporated into their belief system: "And God said unto them, be fruitful, and multiply, and replenish the Earth, and subdue it; and have dominion over the fish of the sea, and over the fowl of the air, and over every living thing that moveth upon the Earth" (Genesis 27). Of course, Biblical injunctions to be fruitful and dominate the Earth are with us still. They even seem to infiltrate the prevailing economic policies, of both the left and the right, that never seem to question the desirability of infinite growth and economic expansion. Growth, of course, is fine, but it never proceeds infinitely and it always entails pain.

The ironic paradox is that to be fruitful and multiply, now, we must sing a different cosmic tune, be guided by a wholly other doctrine, and listen to distinct and (at first) strange adages. Only after we come into accord with nature can we grow as a species—both on and off the Earth. Space remains open to Earth, although space welcomes man not as its sole settler but as an integrator and deliverer of Earthly nature. As Calhoun's experiments suggest, the phase of rapid human population growth is just as rapidly coming to its end.

Overpopulation brings dangers. Simple arithmetic tells us that the more people who are born and live, the more there are who are going to die. Because people are still basically tribal, banding into teams and armies, life and death occur increasingly at the levels of populations and cultures and nations as well as the level of "individuals." When stress becomes severe enough, as it is bound to do in dense communities, organisms react. They may do so in many contradictory ways at the same time. Militants who might otherwise be imprisoned can be of great benefit to—and greatly rewarded by—their populations. Relationships change. From the frenzy and chaos of stressed populations, new modes of interaction arise. Relationships shift. Coerced or not, organisms to survive come together in new arrangements—with new conflicts, new angles of cooperation, new habits of comportment, and new pathways of biochemical interaction. Some of these modes of teaming up are successful. The practitioners of these modes stand to survive. In a sense, humankind is at once the collective witness and the main actor in a participatory spectacle of sexual-symbiotic fascination. The whole Earth has been teeming with life for eons. Now, with the subtlest change, it is teaming up, through humanity, in the production of biospheres. This change is so subtle we would not have noticed it had it not been explicitly called to our attention. Though biospheres may determine human destiny, they have only just entered the field of human consciousness.

Springs

In the film "Pumping Iron," body-building champion Arnold Schwarzenegger repeats in his distinctive Austrian accent the advice: "You must *burn* to grow." This applies beyond the realm of musculature enhancement, of course. Any growth entails pain. A child entering adolescence begins to feel a number of so-called "growing pains," both mental and physical. There is a strange discomfort, the confusion of hormone changes in the body, the pain of adjusting to an adult world, as well as the physical growing pains attributed to the stretching of rapidly growing legs. The entrance into maturity is a struggle between conformacy and belonging. It is a change of regime, a metamorphosis one hopes is more like that of the ugly duckling into a beautiful swan than that of an idealistic child into a resigned adult. As we know, however, debilitating drug use and suicide attempts are concentrated in adolescence.

This is not a specious analogy. Lovelock, whom one must consider the world expert on the emerging science of geophysiology with its implications of the possibility of a planetary medicine, has compared the transition between the Archean and Proterozoic Eons to puberty. While traditional geologists squabble over the exact date of this transition, geophysiologists are more interested in the transition itself. The Proterozoic Eon, which began some 2.5 billion years ago, marks a major change in Earth's chemistry, the transition from an atmosphere seasonally poor in free oxygen to a planetary environment in which oxygen gas became a major constituent of the atmosphere and reacted with rocks, such as iron and uranium, in the Earth's crust. As Lovelock explains, the analysis of oxidized rocks in the fossil record may span a fair amount of time, since these resulted from the changeover to an oxidizing environment.

The important fact for the geophysiologist is the change itself. Somewhat like the appearance of breasts in a young woman, which is chemically prompted by an increase in the flux of a pituitary hormone, the appearance of oxidized rocks in the Earth's crust was chemically prompted by the new bacterial ecosystems that released oxygen into the atmosphere. Of course, transitions of the Earth differ from human puberty in that the Earth may metamorphose any number of times.[2] An acquaintance with Earth history and taxonomy presents us with many analogies for the present phase of planetary transition. But whatever we deem most applicable, it seems clear that we are now in the throes of another planetary changeover whose biochemical effects are only beginning to be registered in what will be posterity's fossil record. As oxygen release was the primary cause of the geobiochemical change of regime that occurred in the Archean-Proterozoic transition, so the main principle at work in this latest adolescence is the worldwide spread of commercial products and technological machines engineered by human beings. In particular, the manipulation of metal and plastics in the recursive circulatory metabolism of the biosphere inaugurates a new eon, a new age in the growth of the biosphere as superorganism.

To understand the new phase of the biosphere we have to understand the new role played by technics, by machines. Machines are better understood as outgrowths of the biosphere than as the creations of human beings. For example, I am wearing a battery-powered, digital watch as I write this—not a spring-wound, mechanical one. The popularity of such digital timepieces vindicates Samuel Butler, who, in the words of philosopher Gregory Bateson, was "Darwin's most able critic." Indeed, Butler seems to be history's deepest thinker on the evolution of machines. For example, clocks, Butler wrote, "which certainly at the present time are not diminishing in bulk, will be superseded owing to the universal use of watches, in which case they will become as extinct as ichtysauri, while the watch, whose tendency has for some years been to decrease in size rather than the contrary, will remain the only existing type of an extinct race." In Butler's book *Erewhon* there is another book, or a fragment of another book, called "The Book of Machines."[3] This book within a book was a manifesto, arguing that the people should rise up and take arms against the increasingly powerful race of nonhuman machines. In Erewhon, an anagram of "nowhere," only fragments of "The Book of Machines" remain.

The machines and books of Erewhon are not "nowhere" but are right here. They are in our hands and before our eyes as walkmen, CD players, telephones, computers, and satellites. Outside my window, birds, insects, and flowers are beginning to stir in the first glimmerings of spring. Still more faintly, in geological rather than seasonal time, another spring is stealing across the face of the Earth. This is the spring of technology. The spring of technology does not belong simply to the watches Butler saw replacing grandfather clocks in his time. The spring of technology is also natural; it uncurls like a wave. Honed of metal and polymers, the technological spring spreading over the face of the Earth is not alien but is deeply rooted in the nature of a biosphere that has always been awkwardly groping, and then smoothly incorporating new chemical compounds into the increasingly large scale of its organization.

Through humanity, the biosphere becomes more powerful, more aware of and able to direct its own evolution. The technological metamorphosis of planet Earth humanizes the outdoors. This is the opposite of the naturalization of the indoors that occurs when we decorate the interiors of houses and buildings with potted plants. It is spreading the principles and potential of humanity on a planetary scale. As the human population impinges upon nature's populations, humankind changes and people come into a new accord. We realize that to live—not just "survive"—we must reintegrate. The technology spawned by us must now be pawned for us to save ourselves on a polluted Earth or to escape into space. We are too many and the Earth is too small. We are not planetary stewards but one of countless flocks wandering the biospheric pasture. Selfishness has reached the point where it transforms into its opposite, selflessness. As our vocabulary decomposes we look at the Earth with new eyes.

Shrunk

Human technology reforms the planetary body, creating a new system for all species to use. Among birds, for example, pigeons make use of cities, some swifts nest in chimneys rather than hollow trees, and nighthawks now live on the flat roofs of factories instead of on the ground. House martins, originally adapted to cliff-living, now congregate also on the walls of houses.

International trade and global technology are not just political or social but biological developments. They open opportunities for other organisms and accelerate genetic travel. Insects cross continents in jet planes; microbes have visited the moon inside the suits of astronauts. Any organism can hook into the planetary transportation system we have set up, stowing away in the hollows of apparatus that can never be reserved solely for humans.

Fossil evidence shows that when a land mass connected North and South America in the Pleistocene epoch, animals crossed in both directions, with the result that North American mammals killed off many of their South American relatives. Biologists call this meeting of land masses and consequent animal crossing "the great American interchange." Now we are in the midst of a greater *biospheric* interchange. With supersonic air travel all organisms on Earth are, in principle, afforded transportation at the speed of sound. The shrinking of distances effected by electronic communication and industrial transportation consolidates the Earth. Earth shrinks.

Garbage and pollution also provoke changes for nonhumans. As always, one species' waste is another species' food. As the rest of life dwells with human technology, our connections to "our" technological products will increasingly be intercepted by opportunistic life forms. Our ties to technology will become increasingly hijacked for purposes we neither intended nor foresaw. It is possible to imagine renegade organisms, mutants of those designed to clean up oil spills and plastics, spreading over the face of the technologically metamorphosed globe, feeding, say, on synthetic rubber tires.

Stress signals that there is a problem to be overcome. In the biosphere this often means a lack of accommodation between two or more rapidly growing life forms. The strain we put on the biosphere is a form of bodily pain; our uneasiness with the environment is a signal telling us to change if we want to arrive at health. First we must reduce environmental stress. Then we may bask in ecological harmony. But it may be that true ecological harmony means letting go even of the notion of stress. Such relaxation would be the spiraling movement of the technological spring. It would be the motionless movement, the half-melted face of the materially limited but eternal cosmos. And this would be a strange clockwork indeed.

CHAPTER 11

~

New Bodies

Life's Ends

Ethically, other organisms should not be treated as means to an end, but as ends in themselves. This high regard for other organisms marked the sacred activities of peoples on a less crowded Earth and of present peoples, such as the native tribes of the Amazon who, by offering prayers to the spirits of the animals they eat, show their regard for the nonhuman living environment. From one perspective, the species *Homo sapiens* is being used by the biosphere as an instrument to turn out new organisms—baby biospheres. It is ironic that our treatment of the Earth—of its resources and living organisms as mere means to the ends of serving our pleasure and maximizing our reproductive success as a species—should in the end be so radically turned about. Transcending humanity now means saving humankind only for our abilities to interface with other species in the prelude to life's reproduction and extraterrestrial expansion, and we may be dispensed with as far as our tendency to reproduce only ourselves goes.

Technology refers to the tools used by life to build. But these tools ultimately can become incorporated into the bodies of their users. The hammer becomes part of the hand. We are moving from a world of instrumentation and industry, a world of accumulating slag heaps, to a biospheric technology, a technology whose by-products recycle instead of pile up. The futuristic technologies contemplated by science fiction, of space stations and human expansion to other worlds, begin to look remarkably organic: the off-Earth dwellings will rely not only on water and carbon-based life to recycle but on silicon and metals in computers whose propensities approach ever more closely a resemblance to life.

Life itself, of course, has already used the materials we associate with technology for eons: diatoms and radiolarians use so much silicon in building their tiny shells that the whole ocean is short in the supply of this element. Coccolithophores can be seen from space as patches of calcium carbonate collecting in the ocean. The Egyptian pyramids contain countless fossils of foraminifers, tiny marine rhizopods with calcareous shells. The calcite spar, the clear crystal used in light microscopes, is itself a sediment crystallized from calcium carbonate solutions coming from tiny shells. Bacteria and large microorganisms accumulate a wide variety of materials from manganese to barium to strontium sulfate. There is no escape from the mineralogical creativity, this artistry in rock developing by, with, and through us at the surface of the Earth under the influence of the sun.

That technological products are becoming increasingly lifelike supports Vernadsky's second principle: over time, more and more elements are involved in the process of biotic circulation. If life is a wave, what is crucial is not the materials from which it is composed as much as its self-production and organization. A study of the fossil record shows that, long before the appearance of *Homo sapiens*, a diverse collection of both abundant and rare chemical elements was incorporated into living organization. Part of life seems always to flirt at the edge of conventionally utilizable compounds. Technology represents not so much life as the interaction between life and the matter it is animating. Whatever life touches becomes increasingly organized, lifelike. Then, when no one is looking, new matter crosses the subtle boundary between non-life and life. Formerly "dead" elements become fully integrated into the ancient biospheric circulation. The external shell becomes the internal support. Life's house becomes its body, and then this new body reaches around itself to create a new house, which will become a new body. The process never ends. Taken as a whole, the act of connections being established by life's body to bring in and incorporate its house is what we call technology.

Tools and Tool Kits

In a semiserious evolutionary burlesque, Butler suggested that mankind is a walking tool kit or workshop fashioned for itself by "a piece of very clever slime."[1] From Butler's perspective—which, in many ways, is that of evolutionary biology taken to its logical conclusions—we ourselves are a technology, the baroque craftwork of uncouth microbes.

We may dismiss such characterizations as undeserved, a selling short of the nobility of men and women. We may scoff at the notion that the human nervous system is a technological switchboard or control panel operated by massive colonies of ancient life forms. We may laugh at the suggestion that each of us represents the hard armor, the urban metropolis, and the mechanical, thinking, and communications apparatus of an elementary horde. But, even if we hold out for a view of men and women loftier than Butler's "tool kit for slime," we are confronted with evidence that evolution of *Homo sapiens* from ape ancestors was not incidentally affected but crucially spurred by technology. Were it not for our handling of the uncertain physiology beyond our skin, we would never have evolved. Anthropogenesis, the development of humanity, depended on prehuman biotechnologies.

Traces of technology are associated with some of the oldest surviving remains of human settlements. Although a tool is really whatever you name a tool—one may pick one's teeth, however impolitely, not only with a toothpick but with a match or a fingernail—certain objects are so often used for discrete purposes that eventually they become associated with certain functions or purposes even when stationary or unused. The shoe we instantly associate with the stockinged foot, and the screw with the screwdriver, even though the former may be used to hammer a nail and the latter is often employed as a clumsy chisel or crowbar. But there could have been invisible tools; most fruits and sticks employed as tools by apes would have decayed without betraying their presence in the fossil record. Although our ancestors, grabbing and dropping tropical tree parts in their forest homeland, may have tossed unripe fruit at their enemies or prey or used dead twigs like limbs to shake distant branches—or to pick the pulp from between their thick molars while surveying the arboreal scene—one would not expect a record of such tools. Since they are organic, they decay. Even preserved, they would show little evidence of having been used as tools.

Stone tools, on the other hand, tend to remain. They are known from Omo, Ethiopia, and date back 2.4 million years. These first tools may be signs of *Homo habilis,* the first of the three species of the human genus (followed by *Homo erectus* and *Homo sapiens*). But, as with the garbage heaps of today, our tools from the beginning may have been more prevalent than ourselves: no *Homo habilis* bones are found at the site in Ethiopia. Tools used by ape-people may precede the human species, belonging to the upright "apes" with chimplike brains that some think evolved not only into early humans but also into the large vegetarian apes *Australopithecus robustus* and *Australopithecus bosei.* Beginning an estimated 2 million years ago, an underground cave complex in South Africa known as Swartkrans collected animals that fell into it including the oldest well-preserved hand bones belonging to the robust australopithecines; a new analysis of these bones suggests that these ape-people, though they are not directly on the line to modern humans, were dextrous enough to grasp and hone stone tools.[2]

Human Cannonballs

As a lever can help lift a heavy object, so tools in general may have acted as an anthropogenic lever, lifting ape-people out of their animality into the beginnings of human being.

We have gone back over 2 million years to the origin of humans and seen that what are apparently the tools of *Homo habilis* predate fossil finds of its bones. Other evidence suggests that the use of tools may extend still further into our past. According to William Calvin, a neurophysiologist at the University of Washington in Seattle, the one feature we can truly say is "human" is not our toolmaking, language, or culture, but our handedness.[3] Other animals use tools. Sea otters smash shellfish on their abdomens while floating on their backs and even swim with the appropriately sized rocks—specially chosen "shell openers" tucked under their arms. Other animals may have language or at least its rudiments: whales and dolphins call each other in the ocean, and even dogs, cats, and birds seem to be able to understand some words and communicate with a limited vocabulary of gestures. Indeed, according to semiotician Thomas Sebeok of the University of Indiana, symbionts must stay in language-like communication merely to survive; biochemicals convey meaning in the pragmatic sense. Some animals even have culture, as in the honeybee societies with their workers and queens or the often-told example of the English tits, small birds that learned and spread among themselves the technique of pecking open the foil tops of English milk bottles and sipping up the milk. As Philip Morrison has pointed out, the ability to build an arch, held by some Western pedants to be the distinguishing mark of a civilization, is accomplished routinely by and for termite colonies. But of all vertebrates only humans, according to Calvin, are predominantly right-handed.

Handedness evolved with specialization of the brain (the left side in right-handed people), a human process that could have become prominent in human populations as our ancestors killed small, quick game by throwing stones. Brain studies have led to the characterization of the left hemisphere of the human brain as "linguistic," "linear," and "verbal." In Calvin's story of human origins, tool using in the form of throwing stones is crucial. Moreover, becoming effective right-handed killers was a prerequisite for story-telling itself.

Of all motor skills, "ballistic" techniques such as rock throwing, javelin (or spear) heaving, bat (or club) swinging, and lasso whirling are activities most strongly associated with the right hand. Rapidly coordinated arm and hand movements such as throwing, clubbing, swinging, and whipping are all similar and differ from fine-motor tasks done primarily with the fingers. The swinging arm motions also differ in being more closely associated with the right hand: while only 77 percent of us thread a needle with the right hand, 88.24 percent hammer, 89.34 percent swing a racket, and 89.47 percent throw a ball with the right hand.

Although most people have never enrolled in a class in calculus, we all pass with flying colors when we aim and throw a rock at a moving target: even "unmathematical" individuals can plot trajectories and project the path of moving objects. Calculating the movement of the arm, the release point of the fingers, and the relative motion of the object to be hit is a very complex mathematical operation. Yet it is done subliminally, with behind-the-scenes genetic know-how. It requires not conscious calculation but instinct, perhaps even the desire to injure or kill.

Calvin suggests that ancestral success in killing small game may have induced something like a computer revolution inside the brains of our ape ancestors. At the same time, as nature bred for bigger and better genetic calculators in one hemisphere, other parts of the brain, controlling subsidiary or even unrelated functions, would have improved. For example, our right hand, associated with the left side of the brain, is associated with language. Linguistic skills may have "come along for the ride," growing out of the more elementary need to procure food. Due to our twofold symmetry, if the throwing-talking side of the brain were selected for, the other side of the brain—with its own distinct abilities—would also have increased in volume.

Calvin and colleague Joan Lockard further speculate that our present right-handedness derives not so much from the advanced throwing techniques of "killer males" but from mothers. Calvin and Lockard suggest that, contrary to common belief, our ancestors may have been largely solitary hunters. If so, mothers, armed with a stone in one hand, would have had to carry their infants on the other side—the left side, where the sound of the thumping heart, reminiscent of the womb and close to the left nipple and breast, would soothe potentially disruptive babies into silence, leaving their mothers free to hunt. Today, from 75 to 80 percent of mothers are estimated to cradle their infants with the left arm.

Small mammals and birds were difficult to catch by creeping up and bludgeoning them with a stick or club. So their predators discovered "action at a distance": by hurling stones our ancestors stunned small game into submission. The animals weren't adapted to fleeing "inanimate" predators such as stones. We use versions of this methodology today when we play basketball or ride a bicycle through traffic. (The numbers of mammals run over by cars shows that they have not evolved to cope with the dangers of rapidly moving cars in the short period of time they have had to learn to do so.) Early humans would have survived not by the skin of their teeth but by the wisdom of their trajectories. MIT computer expert Marvin Minsky in his book *Society of Mind* has shown how hard it is to get a machine to do something as apparently simple as building a tower from children's blocks. Calibrating the trajectory of projectiles in order to kill a small animal is much harder. Yet our "meat machines" (Minsky's phrase for the human brain) figure it out implicitly. They are rich in the "programs" necessary to project just where thrown objects will wind up. According to Calvin, the evolution of these brain programs within the left hemisphere led to the sort of linearity we use in all language, and especially in telling stories. The tossed stone is a piece of rock put in a state of animation at the traditional limits of the human body. But it is precisely the extension of the human body through tool use that makes us so valuable—and dangerous—a geosymbiotic mechanism.

The fossil record shows that australopithecines ancestral to humans were already walking upright 3 million years ago despite having pint-sized brains some one-third the size of ours. But 2 million years ago, with the evolution of *Homo erectus* from the four-foot tall tropical ape *Australopithecus afarensis*, brains became bigger. Perhaps stone throwing played a part in this intracranial expansion. Faster, more accurate throwing may have meant a specific increase in those neurons governing unconscious mathematics. At a very early point, apes would have been diverted onto a "technological track," becoming progressively more adept at "predicting the future" and gauging the effects of manipulating their external environment.

The areas controlling both motor skills (as in rock throwing) and oral-facial musculature (as in speech) are usually located near to each other in the left side of the brain: spoken language may be an unintended offshoot of neural circuitry originally honed for accuracy in throwing rocks. On the other side of the brain, the "unspecialized," "spatial," and "synoptic" abilities attributed to the right side of our brains—purportedly crucial in aesthetic and literary achievements—may have arisen fortuitously as a by-product of brute survival. (Our symmetrical bilateral body shape is so deeply rooted in our embryological development that it is unlikely one side of our brain could shrink even if it were a positive hindrance to the one that was directly selected for). On the other hand (a telltale expression), there is something questionable about any explanation of the origins of language from within language. Mathematician Kurt Gödel showed that it is inherently impossible to prove within the framework of a set of axioms whether certain propositions derived from these axioms are true or false; it is even impossible to figure out which are the undecidable propositions. But it is not just mathematics. In general, systems are not decidable, visualizable from *within*. A fish cannot fully understand its world of water until it crawls outside and looks back at it—until it becomes a human being. A three-year-old uses the grammar of language without being able to explain the way words fit together. Many clues, such as those found in Calvin's intriguing tale, suggest a kind of conspiracy between linear thought and language. And it is linear thought, of course, that puts certain things *first* in an order of importance. Linear thought loves first causes and ultimate principles; it loves the symbolism of the border and the end. Yet linear thought, as epitomized by lines of type, which, according to Calvin, can be traced to selective breeding of parts of the brain involved in protolinguistic rock-throwing calculations, will never understand itself from within the structure of a story—even an evolutionary story, supported with lots of evidence. Heidegger called language the house of being. It is a house we cannot escape.

Finally—to finish the irreducibly paradoxical story of language's origin when it is language that gives birth to stories—Calvin notes that knocking flakes off flint to make points and blades employs an overhand motion, a modification of the gesture used in throwing. It would have been a smooth transition from rock throwing to sharpening flint-tipped spears. And flying sparks, cast off from banging at rocks, might have led not only to occasional burning leaves but also to flashes of insight on how to start, control, and use fires. Stripping the story of our usual human-centered viewpoint, we might say that technology produced itself through anthropogenic encephalization. Rocks, in other words, transformed clumsy apes into dextrous humans; minerals used fire-starting as a tool to melt themselves into the shape of machines. Our ancestors were pyrotechnically invented and *used* by the biosphere as it expanded its resources and the materials of its body.

Menaces

When "we" contemplate the great effects technology has had on our survival in the past, on our ideas and perceptions, and on the lives of our descendents, we begin to see that it is a phenomenon not so much of man, as of life. Samuel Butler realized this by 1863. Born in Nottingham, England, the "transbiological" thinker sailed to New Zealand in 1859. Four years later, when he was twenty-seven, he began what he himself considered to be his first mature writing on the implications of evolution. The writings consisted of two newspaper articles; the first, written under the pseudonym "Cellarius," declared that a new kingdom had appeared on the surface of the Earth that had supervened the animal kingdom, just as the animal kingdom had overcome the vegetable kingdom. "Cellarius," impressed by the vast development of this formerly unrecognized group of mechanical life forms, traced the staggering array of its modern forms (which for Butler meant devices such as the steam engine) "to the earliest primordial types of mechanical life," such as the wedge, the inclined plane, the screw, the pulley, and, ultimately, "to the lever itself." Just like animals, some machines have rudimentary organs that are no longer functional but were used by their ancestors; because of the more rapid rate of human than of natural selection, however, such organs are only rarely found in mechanical devices.

Worrying that human masters of the mechanical race would find it profitable to have the contraptions propagate themselves, "Cellarius" saw forward to a time still further ahead when machines would take control of their own reproductive organs and ultimately make their masters into slaves. Butler's droll alter ego advocated that concerned citizens begin to organize to ward off any such possibility.

Broached here is a theme with which we have by now, in the "information age," become quite familiar: machine menace. It is a nineteenth-century version of the anxiety that machines, even if only many-geared automatons or steam-powered robots, will take over. "Cellarius" ended his piece with the plea that all reasonable men should realize the truth of his philosophical convictions and, realizing that truth, all true patriots of the species should unite in a war to the death against the cursed machines. But even this, he feared, may be futile. For "we have raised a race of beings whom it is beyond our power to destroy" and "we are not only enslaved but are absolutely acquiescent in our bondage." As in Mary Wollstonecraft Shelley's *Frankenstein*, the human creator becomes victim to his technological creation.

We cannot equate "Cellarius" with Butler's full insight into the nature of technological evolution, however. In an article entitled *Lucubratio Ebria*, Butler took issue with his persuasive alias, cogently disputing his literary other.

He countered "Cellarius" with the following argument. The limbs of the lower animals were not, he wrote, modified by any act of deliberation on their part but "by forces which seem insensate to the pain which they inflict, but by whose inexorably beneficent cruelty the brave and strong keep coming to the fore, while the weak and bad drop behind and perish." In other words, the Darwinian theory of evolution by natural selection explained our remote ancestors—but this changed when at last "human intelligence stole like a late spring upon the mimicry of our semi-simious ancestry, the creature learnt how he could, of his own forethought, add extra-corporaneous limbs to the members of his body and become not only a vertebrate mammal, but a vertebrate machinate [sic] mammal into the bargain." Man, Butler synopsized, during his "gorilla-hood" had carried a stick for so long that he learned to walk upright with it, and later he used it both to beat his younger brothers and as a lever. Perceiving the "moral government" of nature, man began to "symbolize it, and to this day our poets and prophets still strive to symbolize it more and more completely." Taking sticks from trees, using the arboreal environment as a workshop from which we could add to our bodies ready-made limbs of many types, we were able to epitomize the slow, Darwinian evolution of simpler creatures, updating our body plan not by evolutionary trial and error but by whim.

In *Lucubratio Ebria*, Butler contrasts the "machinate" nature of man with other animals such as the opossum, elephant, or bee, who "has never fairly grasped the notion of tacking on other limbs to the limbs of her own body." No race on Earth, he points out, not even the "lowest Australian savage" is without tools; indeed, without extra-corporaneous limbs men would not even be men at all.

> It is a mistake, then, to take the view adopted by a previous correspondent of this paper [himself, writing two years before as Cellarius,]; to consider the machines as identities, to animalize them, and to anticipate their final triumph over mankind. They are to be regarded as the mode of development by which human organism is most especially advancing, and every fresh invention is to be considered as an additional member of the resources of the human body.

Human beings are elevated not so much by our flesh and blood, our consciousness, perceptions, and language as by "the deliberate invention of such unity of limbs as is exemplified by the railway train—that seven-leagued foot which five hundred may own at once." We are not simply the children of our parents. We are also "children of the plough, the spade, and the ship; we are children of the extended liberty and knowledge which the printing press has diffused."

The Richest Flesh

Butler explored the consequences of technology, of our "external anatomy" as if with the fresh and seeringly ironic eyes of a visitor from another galaxy—one having no preconceived notions of what it is that makes us human:

By the institutions and state of science under which a man is born it is determined whether he shall have the limbs of an Australian savage or those of a nineteenth-century Englishman. The former is supplemented with little save a rug and a javelin; the latter varies his physique with the changes of the season, with age, and with advancing or decreasing wealth. If it is wet he is furnished with an organ which is called an umbrella and which seems designed for the purpose of protecting either his clothes or his lungs from the injurious effects of rain. His watch is of more importance to him than a good deal of his hair, at any rate than his whiskers; besides this he carries a knife, and generally a pencil case. His memory goes in a pocket book. He grows more complex as he becomes older and he will then be seen with a pair of spectacles, perhaps also with false teeth and a wig; but, if he be a really well-developed specimen of the race, he will be furnished with a large box upon wheels, two horses, and a coachman.

As Butler developed his perception of man as the "machinate mammal" he came to the conclusion that evolutionary differences of race between, say, African and European or native American and Chinese were trivial compared to the differences between rich and poor. Today rich people can go virtually wherever they want at a moment's notice, but the poor are generally prevented by their lack of financial support from traveling further than their legs or a bus will take them. The affection we lavish on rich celebrities is simply a result of the respect we feel for their more complex organization. It is similar to the feelings of a dog toward its owner, "and is not infrequently manifested in a similar manner." In Butler's time technological humanity was not quite as advanced as it is today:

He alone possesses the full complement of limbs who stands at the summit of opulence, and we may assert with strictly scientific accuracy that the Rothschilds are the most astonishing organisms that the world has ever seen. For to the nerves or tissues, or whatever it be that answers to the helm of a rich man's desires, there is a whole army of limbs seen and unseen attachable: he may be reckoned by his horse-power—by the number of foot-pounds which he has money enough to set in motion. Who, then, will deny that a man whose will represents the motive power of a thousand horses is a being very different from the one who is equivalent but to the power of a single one?

Perhaps Butler's second article is closer to his true views, his considered opinion. In his personal notes he developed the notion of the body as a walking tool box or workshop fashioned for itself by "a piece of very clever slime" over long experience. As a cotton factory is not so much the machinery and building but the goods it turns out to be made into clothes for people to wear, so we people are only very partially our physical body, and should think of ourselves rather in terms of the work we do and the effect we have on the world, which could last a long time after we are gone. This is an elegantly biospheric perspective; Butler looks at humans the way Vernadsky looks at soil or Darwin describes earthworms. His perspective is redolent with a natural history that defines the human not at the borders of our skin but in terms of our effects on the environment, of our input and output, of what comes into contact with and moves through us. Indeed, for Butler our true life really begins only after we die, when our work has the opportunity to make an impact, as Shakespeare's did in his plays, which are more fully and widely known today than they were during his lifetime. Furthermore, the work we do in the world, creating art and technology with our wit and limbs, uses the same skills that were used in the invention of ourselves. (Our body is a form of technology, and we can get a feeling for this when we think of our legs carrying us somewhere or when we "throw our fist into a man's face as though it were a stick we had picked up to beat him with. For the moment, our fist is hardly 'us,' but it becomes 'us' again as we feel the resistance it encounters from the man's eye. Anyway, we can only chuck about a part of ourselves at a time, we cannot chuck the lot—and yet I do not know this, for we may jump off the ground and fling ourselves on to a man.") Are tools a form of life sired by, but separate from, humans? Or are tools and machines organs external to the human body?

Wireless Nerves

In the 1960s Canadian communications theorist Marshall McLuhan articulated a perception of technology that reflected the widespread changes that have occurred since the time of Butler. In many ways the devices that Butler spoke of as being so highly organized—steam-driven railway trains, ships, and the like—are already outmoded. They have given way to air traffic, fiber optics, and microwave ovens; the world views of Newtonian physics and Lord Kelvin have been swept away by a new scientific universe of X-rays, nuclear energy, sound recording, transistors, lasers, masers, transistors, superconductors, radio, radar, and radioactive dating.

It is this world of electronics and communication at the speed of light that so impressed McLuhan. He perceived it not as a bunch of isolated scientific developments but as an instantaneous social nervous system. The medium of electricity altered the very nature of communication itself, conforming meaning to its expression in electronic information. With the emphasis of Western culture shifting from Europe to America (and from America to the Pacific basin), empires shrink into hamlets and the planet becomes smaller not in a physical sense but in the sense that events on one side of the world can be "gossiped" to parts thousands of miles away by means of electronic media. One is not even aware of all the subtle influences communicated by television; at the same time, huge groups of people are simultaneously exposed to identical visual stimuli. Attention is focused communally. As everybody knows each other in a small town, so the "small-townness" of electronically transmitted information induces everything to become instantly related to everything else.

Although in his writings McLuhan continually contrasted the fragmentation of tools in the mechanical age of Butler with the new instantaneous character of electronic devices, he too has intuited the (super) organismic nature of technology:

It has often been said by engineers that, as information levels rise, almost any sort of material can be adapted to any sort of use. This principle is the key to the understanding of electric automation. In the case of electricity, as energy for production becomes independent of the work operation, there is not only the speed that makes for total organic interplay, but there is, also, the fact that electricity is sheer information that, in actual practice, illuminates all it touches. Any process that approaches instant interrelation of a total field tends to raise itself to the level of conscious awareness, so that computers seem to "think." In fact, they are highly specialized at present, and quite lacking in the full process of interrelation that makes for conscious-

ness. Obviously, they can be made to simulate the process of consciousness, just as our electric global networks now begin to simulate
the condition of our central nervous system. But a conscious computer
would still be one that was an extension of our consciousness, as a
telescope is an extension of our eyes, or as a ventriloquist's dummy
is an extension of the ventriloquist.[4]

Just as, one assumes, our consciousness is an extension of the biosphere, or what Vernadsky called the "Earth-solar system"—or, indeed,
the universe at large.

Like an ancient nautilus drawing calcium from its kidney stone to
fashion its shell, civilization's tools represent the point at which alien
matter is absorbed into biotic circulation. We play phylogenetic hide-and-
seek. Through humanity the biosphere is "flirting" with the cosmic environment, turning it to human purposes, eventually incorporating environment as technology and prostheses into humanlike forms.

But this is nothing new: the "outside" of our ancestors—such as the
toxic salt calcium phosphate that they had to dump outside their cells so
it wouldn't jam their metabolism—is now our "inside": the human skeleton. We would not even be human without such metamorphosed solid
waste sites, which our ancestors so cleverly put to use. The process of
bioassimilation, of incorporating the old into the new, goes on unceas-
ingly. The addition of metals and plastics, wires and wheels, is simply
where life is at this late stage in the game.

CHAPTER 12

~

Extinction

A Tissue for the Pox

"The earth is beautiful," inscribed Friedrich Wilhelm Nietzsche upon a piece of paper torn from the very living body he was discussing, "but it has a pox called man." Photographs from space bear Nietzsche out. The round blue sky and oceans of Earth the planet are beautiful, as beautiful as a jewel, a liquid sphere of planetary sapphire. But here on the ground, in the thick of it, things are dirtier. Gas tanks contaminate the subterranean water supply; oil spills and medical wastes spoil the coastlines; livestock and farmworkers touch pesticides; acid rain and foulwater algae kill fish and local fishing declines; we have problems of air pollution, nuclear waste disposal, and so on. Typical supermarket produce includes daminozide-laced apples, grapes with methyl bromide, chlorothalonil-infested carrots, milk contaminated with aflatoxin, and potatoes exposed to chlorpropham and aldicarb. Over two decades ago DDT was found in amazingly remote regions, such as in eggs of Siberian eagles, indicating that life on Earth is so incestuous—so interwoven in nutritional latticeworks of predators and prey—that no organism can effectively escape toxins once they are introduced into the biospheric system. More recently, the toxin dioxin has been found in toilet tissue. One might well wonder whether traces of such poisons would be discovered by a chemical analysis of this very page.

Species are now dying off at the fastest clip since the Cretaceous period 60 million years ago, at which time all the dinosaurs as well as many other species became extinct. If man was kicked out of Eden for eating from the tree of knowledge, at least the apple was not laced with Alar, as are many today. In the summer of 1970 an inconspicuous fungus called *Helminthosporium maydis* spread from Florida to the Midwest corn belt, destroying 15 percent of what would have been the harvest. The corn leaf blight spread so rapidly because most of the corn in the United States— 71 percent of it—was the result of six inbred parent kinds. Four-fifths of the corn was sterile, containing the same Texas male-sterile cytoplasm, a trait favored by plant breeders because it prevents corn plants from pollinating naturally and thus reverting to less productive wild types. Because only diversity prevents outbreaks of disease, the new monocultures had to be designed to be resistant to the most common pests. Money poured into the technological production and application of pesticides, fungicides, herbicides, and insecticides. There is no question that the miracle corn was plentiful and tasty: the fungus *H. maydis* sure thought so, and no fungicide prevented its spread at the expense of this monocrop. (Agriculturists were ultimately successful at breeding in resistance to the unforeseen fungus.)

This new dependence on machines, pesticides, genetic engineering, and the whole technological gestalt is self-reinforcing. Diversity is old. Freeman Dyson at a meeting to honor the late physicist Heinz Pagels spoke of the destiny of the human species. Dyson mentioned waking up from a mugging with a curious sense of relief, even on the edge of death, with the lifeblood oozing out of him—he felt as if he were a leaf floating off into eternity. He spoke of the age of the species, of the culture, of the family—all of which are older than the individual who must often divide his allegiance among them. On the one hand, nature has given us greed and virtually limitless self-regard; on the other, a love for the grass, the leaves, animals, and trees. Dyson told how the emotions, presumably rooted in the ancient part of the brain known as the limbic system, which we share with all mammals, are older than the cerebral cortex, the center of our rational, human, and scientific activities. Of course, an emotional tie lies at the root of our "biophilia," Wilson's name for our innate serenity in the presence of ancestral ecosystems. We must not lose, Dyson says, the limbic bond to the biosphere: the pleasure to be gained by planting trees to counter the greenhouse effect, by returning to Earth, falling in with nature. As the tools of the biosphere we find a new happiness, and an old serenity; and if the difference between the wisdom of the body and the wisdom of the mind is illustrated by the difference between the way a plant grows and the way a botanist describes the growth of a plant, then the biosphere, oldest and broadest of the unconsciously thinking physiologies, is, no doubt, the most wise.

The anthropocentric counterexample to a global-centered human future Dyson brings up in the figure of parents a generation or so hence who select the desired genetic traits of their offspring. Technically selected, bioengineered children would, Dyson surmises, be attractive and beautiful and successful in the short run but dangerous for humanity as a whole. The specter of human breeding is ominous. Society has evolved integrated with nature; the last thing we need is a fresh crop of *human* monoculture; society needs its specialized parts, we might say, the way an animal requires tissues, or an organism, organs. Dyson ended his reflection by musing that perhaps, as he lay there flat on the streets of Washington, he had seen a glimpse of the face of Gaia.

But the dangers of loss of diversity are not confined to the fields of agriculture and science fiction: environmentalist Norman Myers projects that by the year 2000 A.D. 100 species will become extinct per *day*, mainly due to the destruction of forests in the Amazon and the loss of animal habitats that quickly ensues. For example, forests have been cut down in Mexico and Central America to raise the cattle that provide fast-food for Americans; when the 150 or so species of North American songbirds fly south to Central America and the Caribbean each summer, they find their wintering grounds degraded. Each spring fewer return north to breed. Projecting the slowdown in their return, about half the several billion songbirds are estimated to be gone by the turn of the century. As Myers writes: "We are well aware of the main mechanisms of extinction, especially those which derive from human activities. But these mechanisms tend to be studied in isolation from each other. We know much less . . . about the dynamic interplay. . . . This means that a large-scale elimination of species may occur even sooner than some observers anticipate."[1] Long-term security for global humanity depends not so much on military protection from each other as on sustaining biological resources. The interconnections of species are so complex, however, that some fear the death of even a few key species could lead to the unravelling of the whole biological fabric that supports human beings. Even now, elephants, tigers,

and bears—many of the so-called charismatic metazoans—are in danger
of extinction. These are the favorite zoo animals of our youth, feared and
respected by our ancestors, and they are disappearing from this planet.
Yet it would be presumptuous to say that we understand the planetary
body well enough to know how to go about prescribing an overall treatment, assuming, of course, that the disappearance of most large mammals,
from the vantage point of the long-term survival of planetary life as a
whole is even a problem. As far as we know, the rise and demise of
humanity—interrupted only by siring (self-maintaining) technology—is
part of the normal course of life's planetary phase. Without a basis for
comparison, we float from event to event in what Milan Kundera calls
"the lightness of being." We have no other "patients" around to study
the etiology and symptoms and potential treatment of planetary disease.
We can operate only by intuition. And since world history is not a re-
peatable experiment, planetary treatment remains firmly within the realm
of art as opposed to that of science.

Lovelock writes:

> As in hypochondria the real problem is not that these global maladies
> are unreal, but the uncertainty over whether the present symptoms
> are prodromal of disaster or whether they are no more than the growing
> pains of the world. . . . Intelligent hypochondriacs do not consult a
> biochemist or a molecular biologist about their worries; they go instead
> to a physician. A good physician knows that hypochondria often masks
> a real ailment quite different from the one imagined by the patient.
> Could it be that our very deep concern about the state of the world
> is a form of global hypochondria? . . . What would be the qualifi-
> cations of a planetary physician? . . . The recognition by Paracelsus
> that "the poison is the dose" was a physiological enlightenment still
> to be discovered by those environmentalists who seek the unattainable
> and pointless goal of zero for pollutants.[2]

Technology has come from us and we have come from the Earth. It
is a natural phenomenon. We have seen the global spread of the ac-
coutrements of the industrial revolution, a sweeping movement from creek
and pastures to concrete curbs and asphalt parking lots, from blue skies
filled with languid clouds to rush-hour air traffic and omnipresent smog.
Is this stage similar to that of a biotic invasion? Is it like the infectious

phase of a parasite before it has learned not to kill the host upon which its livelihood depends? Technology may be dangerous, but adding technology to nature makes nature stronger and more stable than nature without technology.

Often in evolution, organisms, altered by their association with other organisms, lose parts of themselves. For example, albino plants that live parasitically on other plants have lost the ability to photosynthesize; they undergo photosynthesis by proxy. The gradual atrophy of parts is always a tendency of life in a living environment; organic connections render independent beings that were once self-sufficient and self-contained. The expansion of identity and loss of parts is also underway in the human sphere. Our identity has expanded to include technology: we have lost or are losing the abilities to build fire from sticks, to find our own food, and to live in the earlier human environments to which our limbic systems are still attuned. It is second nature for us now to buy food in supermarkets, which must be stocked by trucks, themselves dependent on gasoline, agricultural machinery, and so on. Not only has the rise in the human population been aided and abetted by our use of technics—and the technical thinking that is the basis of scientific mastery—but no matter how great our nostalgia for our lost habitats, we cannot return to them without forfeiting millions of humans. To maintain anywhere near the current planetary human population requires a maintenance of the world's technological character—the very character we find so disturbing.

Although we deeply depend on modern technology, we are not yet involved in our own evolution and in the technical reworking of our own bodies to the extent that we will be. A "biont" is a biological unit, such as a member of a species; a "technobiont" is a biological entity from which the technological component can no longer be removed, even surgically, without death ensuing. Ours is a "pretechnobiontic" civilization—rich in detachable organs, in umbrellas that you can put down and in cars that you can step out of. But a truly technobiontic civilization is just around the corner. Indeed, it is already partially here, in the form of pacemakers and other still sparsely used medical prostheses without which death would rapidly ensue.

It may well be that the technological components of the biosphere are fated to become perfectly integrated into the Gaian system of global survival—not an adjunct to but a part of life, as natural as can be. In the meantime, however, the Earth is still sick with the high technological fever of humankind. A cybernetic system reacts unstably at the point of stress, as we do when trying to control a car veering out of control along a slippery road. Perhaps the biosphere will be knocked into a new ice age; maybe the Earth will overheat as the greenhouse effect puts us past the point of human habitation. The breaking of biospheric malaria—like fever alternating with chills—could give way to a frozen or jungle world without human beings. A physiological biosphere does not mean that our polluting and disruptive actions will somehow be directly compensated for and the Earth will stay hospitable for human beings; in fact, it may mean precisely the reverse: that a slight planetary change, one we may not notice or be overly concerned with, could alter biogeochemistry in a global way, tipping the biosphere over into a new regime, inhospitable to ourselves among other species. Whereas turning a steering wheel to stay on a road entails negative feedback, there is also positive and runaway feedback, as in the example of the drunken driver hydroplaning out of control until he crashes. A physiological Earth cybernetically amplifies would-be small effects, just as it regulates would-be large ones. That human beings are now spread liberally over the surface of the Earth, inhabiting a wide range of habitats, provides no guarantee, but is at least some insurance, that we will not become extinct as easily as less widely spread species.

No one knows planetary destiny. There is only one Earth, as each of us lives only one life. As Lovelock's language suggests, we don't even know if the effects of our interactions are disease-like perturbations or the highly natural result of a natural process of planetary growth. This lack of understanding is crucial to an understanding of our planetary relation. We literally stand within the biosphere, inside the terrestrial system that circumscribes all our analyses, rendering moot all hopes of a final objectivity. Indeed, even this duality of sickness or technological metamorphosis, with its implicit assumption that the planetary diagnosis must be either benign or malignant, is probably a mistake. If the biosphere is an organism, it is an organism far more complex than we—not necessarily superior, dynamically different, and larger—as we are beyond an amoeba. Never having seen the organism's growth, or witnessed its life cycle, how can we say what is normal? Is the current planetary metamorphosis pathogenic? We are an unknown quantity, trying to ascertain whether we are tumor or organ, mutant or normal, fetus or flash in the pan. The planetary physician is not only a diagnostician but a symptom, the fluke itself. The medical analogy here breaks down, precisely when we realize that nature, unlike the human doctor, treats itself.

Ego into gEo

Let us examine more closely this question of health and stability. Lovelock's Daisyworld models have shown that some mathematical models—those that include realistic environmental variables—demonstrate that diversity does increase stability. This vindicates what some of the practical ecologists have been telling mathematical ones for a long time, only now the practical ecology has been given a mathematical basis, too. In general, the greater the variety of living organisms modeled in Lovelock's computer—organisms such as black, white, and grey daisies, and cows and foxes and rabbits—the greater the unconscious modulation of planetary temperature. With sufficient species even the upsets caused by rapidly evolving viruses and meteorite-based climatic disturbances can be neutralized. Although all this happens in cyberspace—the make-believe, mathematized world of electronic signals—and is concerned only with the stabilization of the single variable, temperature, the correlation between the diversity and vigor of a living system may well apply to the biosphere as a whole. Lovelock's models differ from now passé population ecology models primarily in the attention he has given to feedback from the environment. The growth of organisms in their environment in Lovelockian models affects the environment and subsequent growth of organisms.

Lovelock claims that part of his success has been that he never reads the literature in a subject before beginning experimentation. He has repeatedly mentioned losing interest in Gaia as it develops its own, presumably restrictive, literature. Nonetheless, Lovelock's Daisyworld scenarios vindicate an older tradition in ecology that sees a correspondence between diversity and stability, and Lovelock himself has warned against the "three Cs," namely, cars, cattle, and chainsaws—the use of all of which dangerously reduce global diversity. The environmental threats range from razing rainforests and fatally disrupting habitats of a wide variety of forest communities to make room for cattle grazing and beef production to disrupting the planet's ability to cool itself off. Automobile and other fossil-fuel exhaust produces a blanket of carbon dioxide that traps infrared radiation at the Earth's surface, keeping it warm. According to Lovelock, Gaia may not like it hot since maximum biomass, the richest ecosystems of living organisms, can only exist by taking the carbon from the carbon dioxide in the atmosphere in order to build up their own bodies. Lovelock suggests that presently Gaia may be having the rough equivalent of a "fever," and that ice-age temperatures, which expose the prime real estate of continental shelves by draining the oceans of water to make glaciers, may be more healthy for planetary life as a whole.

Keeping carbon landlocked as living organisms rather than floating freely as carbon dioxide gas in the air would be most desirable, but by driving and thus releasing carbon dioxide in the air we increase the greenhouse effect, which is in essence a planetary fever. Global controls on the burning of fossil fuels, not eating meat, and protecting what amounts to geophysiological organs such as the Amazon rainforest are among the most important personal measures we can take to promote planetary wellbeing. If we act now we may even be able to forestall the industrially induced changeover to a new regime far less hospitable to human life as we know it. By avoiding these three deadly Cs we help preserve biological diversity, the products of which are equivalent to plying the biosphere with the vitamins, minerals, and nutrients it needs to keep itself healthy in its present form. In short, what is good or convenient for us is not necessarily good for the biosphere; but if there is a showdown, the biosphere, which is one-third the age of the universe, qualifies for the adjective immortal far more than humanity does. If the past tells us about the future, the biosphere will survive—even if it is forced to change its entire geophysiology and metamorphose in the process. The prospects for diversity-squandering humankind look bleak by comparison.

Ecologist G. Evelyn Hutchinson explained the stabilizing effect of diversity by roles. A rich ecosystem with many species performing many different functions—"dividing the labor"—is more stable because the functions of individual species are replaceable. An environmental niche is like a company well-stocked with professionals, and the more professionals who can fill in to perform a task, the more assured will be that business's success. A one-man business, by contrast, is riskier because if the single entrepreneur becomes sick or involved in other concerns, no one else may be available to take his or her place. So it is with ecosystems. When one sort of herbivore becomes extinct, another kind expands to feed on the newly available plant food, keeping the biomass stable and preventing the sort of rapid growth we associate with cancer. Like a "deep" sports team with quality players ready to play but held on reserve, the hardiest ecosystems have a multiplicity of feedback systems, where, in case of emergency, one group of organisms can assume another's role.

The research of Soviet biologist M. M. Kamshilov graphically displays this ecological depth. Kamshilov tested the resistance of a variety of communities to the toxic effects of phenolic acid and found that the most complex assemblages most quickly broke down this biologically hazardous substance. Kamshilov added the acid to four different model ecosystems. The first consisted of bacteria, the second of bacteria and aquatic plants, and the third of bacteria, aquatic plants, and mollusks. The fourth consisted of bacteria, aquatic plants, and fish. Although only bacteria can break down phenol into its harmless constituents, the latter-mentioned communities containing fish and mollusks as well as bacteria and plants disintegrated the toxin the fastest.

Kamshilov cites several factors for this phenomenon, including the fact that the waste products of the marine animals are food for the bacteria, thus speeding up disintegration, the healing and fixing process of detoxification. He also noted that as plants and animals were added, microorganisms that feed on bacteria were also included. These microorganisms normally adhering to plant and animal bodies returned the mineral elements used in bacterial growth to the medium, thus further speeding up detoxification. Kamshilov concluded that "the greater the diversity of species the more vigorous is the destruction of the toxic material."[3] Since we are a species introducing many toxins into the biosphere while we systematically destroy biological diversity, Kamshilov's experiments suggest that keeping the biosphere clean—the air fresh, the waters blue—is related not only to pollution control measures but to seemingly unrelated things such as preserving swamps, microbial mats, rainforests, and other locales of great biological diversity.

But if the biosphere acts, due to the continual propagation of its biochemically extremely versatile populations, as a self-adjusting Daisyworld, humanity may nonetheless upset it for humanity. We are capable of disturbing so many systems. One way, for example, that we shake up the planetary ecology is by the decimation we have wreaked upon animal species—those organisms most like ourselves. Unlike past mass extinctions chronicled by paleobiologists in the fossil record, the present mass extinction seems not to have an external cause but clearly to be motivated from within by one virus-like species: humanity. By urbanizing the planet to provide shelter and employment for our own hordes, we systematically rob many once happy—and geophysiologically integrated—species of their habitats, plunging them into the nether reaches of extinction.

It may be instructive, when considering the potential consequences of losing biospheric diversity, to compare the biosphere as a whole to a person afflicted with the HIV virus, showing the first devastating symptoms of AIDS. This is not an invidious comparison for the following reasons: (1) Like the HIV retrovirus, humanity's ill effects on the global organism are not the result of premeditation, but of a certain fortuitous transmutation or "jump," which has allowed us to circumvent normal barriers preventing unfettered growth; (2) As with the HIV virus, humanity does not attack all areas of the environment equally but rather afflicts the environment in what must be its weakest point: its reserve of internal diversity.

The human presence may have reached sufficient numbers to overcome what would normally be the global equivalent to an immune system. This is the storehouse of species themselves. According to the "necessary diversity law," a law held fundamental to cybernetics, a system must attain sufficient internal diversity before it can block internal and external perturbations. If the biosphere is a nonpurposive internally organized system, it may be tolerating humanity as reluctantly as an AIDS victim tolerates the HIV virus. As the retrovirus afflicts the human immune system, so expanding human populations deplete the biospheric stock of internal diversity by being culpable for mass extinctions of nonhuman species. In the aggregate, these nonhuman species may protect the biosphere no less than the immune system guards the individual human body.

Zoologists, evolutionary biologists, paleontologists, and conservationists have already compared the loss of species at human hands, prompted by the need for food, the quest for pelts, or pure savagery, to be the greatest in 65 million years, since the time of the Cretaceous mass extinction that effaced all the dinosaurs. Because species are connected ecologically, when one species becomes extinct many others may fall with it, unravelling like fabric. Let us assume, then, that the biosphere is capable of reacting like a sensitive body to the human attack on or depletion of its internal reserve of genetic diversity. In theory, this internal reserve increases the biosphere's chances of resisting attacks and perturbations. Yet it is precisely the means of resistance that humanity is "attacking." We are blindly interrupting the growth of other species as we strive to increase our own.

However, there is a point in complex systems beyond which strength in numbers begins to backfire. Even if we are the most influential single species on the globe at present (to biospheric control what a conductor is to a symphony), we require a vast suite of other species to maintain ourselves: a conductor cannot generate pleasant sounds from an orchestra composed solely of other conductors. Populations of streptococcus bacteria are normally present on human skin; nonetheless they may, if conditions change, overgrow their natural boundaries and cause visible infections. In a like manner, humanity is overgrowing its natural boundaries. The effects of industry and technology disrupt the biochemistry of the global ecosystem that so far has supported humanity. By killing off other species, *Homo sapiens* affects life in what may be its weakest spot, its Achilles' heel. The effect of humanity on the biosphere may then be tragic to the extreme—not a superficial affliction, but a deep-rooted penetration, a systemic infection, an attack at the Earth's heart, its jugular, its immune system.

Although we want to survive, there is a less anthropocentric view of what we are doing to the biosphere that does not necessarily entail our survival. Our lessening of biological diversity may, in fact, be healthy for the biosphere as a whole, a biosphere that has finally as little regard for our welfare as we do for our normally occurring skin bacteria. Many ecological investigations have discovered that some communities require periodic perturbations to maintain their status. Fire seems destructive to the savanna but ultimately it is necessary and invigorating. In children, milk teeth tissue dies and teeth are shed as a prerequisite to full health and maturity. The spread of humanity changes the rules of the biospheric game as fast as we can learn them. We chaotically alter the entire entrenched biogeochemical structure of the biosphere, and we may be acting not as disease agents but as catalysts in the changeover to a new planetary environment. From a planetary medicine perspective, the technological products with which we ply the biosphere may act simultaneously like poisons and hormones. A catalyst is a compound that brings about chemical reactions while not itself altering. Compounds we introduce into the biosphere may be toxic to us as their human producers even as they spur the biosphere on to new heights. Once again, puberty seems an appropriate analogy. Like testosterone or anabolic steroids in a young man, the geophysiological outcome of the introduction of new chemicals may be an increase in biospheric strength, global poisoning, or both. We must clearly distinguish between the health of the biosphere and the health of humankind. While our health depends upon a robust biosphere, the biosphere in no way depends on us. We hang on like the streptococcus bacteria.

*   *   *

The most hardy and robust life form may be one that integrates not only a larger number of species but technological components as well. A person with a telephone, who can call an ambulance, is more likely to survive than a person lacking such equipment. The appearance of cyborganic beings with bows and arrows, with televisions and cars, ironically succeeds in perpetuating not only the beings but the complex of devices upon which technologically integrated humans depend. These tools or technology are still a kind of offshoot or excrement at the margins of planetary recirculation. But their integration into a food-waste-food cycle would represent a technological strengthening of the biosphere as a whole, and on the plane of consciousness it would represent a transformation of anthropocentrism, of the human ego into a transhuman "geo."

The biospheric potential of human tools looms ever larger. For example, California Institute of Technology geologist Eugene Shoemaker advocates preparing weapons systems to destroy meteorites before they collide with Earth; if military technology were systematically diverted from national interest to panhuman ecology, one could claim that technology had enhanced the survival of the biospheric whole. Redirected, nuclear warheads could enhance rather than endanger the mutual survival of Earth's inhabitants, human and nonhuman alike, by blasting incoming "planetismals." As with evolving organisms, the purposes for which complex technological systems are originally devised may be, to use evolutionary jargon, "exapted," reworked from their original uses and honed for other purposes. In their story *The Greening of Mars*, Lovelock and Michael Allaby imagine a future in which missiles designed to carry nuclear weapons are used to carry fluorocarbons to Mars instead; although subsequent calculations prove the plan unfeasible, the idea is a good one. It is also possible to imagine bombarding Mars to create craters so deep atmospheric pressure at the bottom (eight to thirteen kilometers) would be similar to Earth, as part of a preliminary step in the process of terraformation; this suggestion was made by James Oberg in his book *New Earths*.

When one thinks of the inherent phallic symbolism of missiles, which have even been called "impotent" rather than ineffective, it seems poetically fitting that their violent role might be subverted and redirected toward one of fertility and peace. Such a turnabout would demonstrate that the artifacts of human culture can serve many purposes at once in the elegant manner of evolutionary structures. We have the possibility of a wholesale restructuring of humanity in its role within the biosphere. Would this not be like the irreducible ambiguity of our own human body, whose mouth serves to eat and to talk, whose nose both smells and breathes, whose genitals economically double for the distinct tasks of urination and procreation? The amazing body of Gaia reworks itself; nature refashions and returns. In the broadening or redirection of technology toward all life, Earth life enters a new phase, a phase in which technology becomes as important for the biosphere as it has been and still is for each of us as technologically dependent humans. Thinking less of purpose than of fate or destiny, one can anticipate here a metamorphosis of colossal dimensions, one that sweeps along humanity and shows it up as dispensable, transitory, a mere ecological phase preparatory to extraterrestrial expansion.

In the long term, technology can be expected to add to life's overall vigor and stability. Computers will probably be included in those sophisticated ecosystems with the greatest powers of detoxification. Encapsulated, robotic ecosystems are far better equipped to adapt to radically new territories, not only in space but on Earth. Maintaining a home aquarium discontinuous with the surrounding ecosystem requires technology: after the proper concentrations of salinity are set up and the chlorine of tap water is removed, a rugged "pioneer" species such as damsel fish and brine shrimp must be introduced. The bacteria naturally dwelling on the surface of such an organism expand to inhabit the tank, where they proceed to metabolize the harmful ammonia normally found in fish waste into less harmful nitrite and then to nitrate; still, from 1 to 10 percent of the water of the tank must usually be replenished on a monthly basis to prevent build-up of nitrogenous wastes. Later, depending on the expertise of the pisciculturist, different compatible combinations of fish can be introduced into the tank.

The point is that it is virtually impossible to recreate the natural environment of the ocean in a small setting without a mixture of biology and technology: it is the meeting ground, the mixture of these two uneasily cohabiting partners, that announces the advent of a more expansive life at home and in the stars. In aquaria, filtration and aeration systems are necessary to ensure adequate amounts of oxygen in the water and to avoid dangerous accumulation of nitrogen and metabolic wastes. Heaters are sometimes necessary and the water must periodically be changed so that hazardous concentrations of ammonia and nitrate do not build up. Carbonates must be added to counter acidity in the tank arising from metabolic wastes of the fish or other inhabitants. Without technology, indoor aquariums would be impossible. And yet a much older encapsulatory technology—complex carbon and calcium compounds—permitted life to come to land in the first place.

Technology's virulent quality may be extremely destructive in the short term, but technology may be like a pioneer kingdom—a new entity stealing across the Earth, awakening allergic species and sensibilities in a planetary spring. From the biospheric point of view, technology's virulence cannot last: the deadliest organisms destroy their own resources and with them their own chances for continued survival. We therefore may recognize technology's dangerous characteristics as a sign of its power, not of its inherent evil. This power gives us the word, the verb "to live," the inevitability of climatic change, cosmic springtime. Cleverness now resides in devising means of technological jujitsu, of flipping and reorienting technology, sending it flying in directions other than those for which it may have originally been intended. Organs have multiple functions. In the schism of life, organisms may become organs or seeds of superorganisms. Diverting missile launch systems to the task of making Mars into a fertile anaerobic swamp would be using the same technology to spread rather than to destroy life.

At home, technology, far from desensitizing and destabilizing biochemically living communities, could be used to stabilize and sensitize them in a new planetary order. One might say that spy satellite technology already has been refashioned, reoriented toward biospheric introspection, watching over the planetary community in the monitoring of agriculture and weather—eyes not only of nations but of and over the Earth. Coming in the short term we stand to face the trials of a possibly painful biospheric reorganization. But in the long term such reorganization could very well lead to greater ecological stability. In the difficult interim our responsibility should be to become as shining an example of life on Earth as Earth is of life in space.

CHAPTER 13

~

The Dividing

Birth is a large concept. It need not be restricted to mammals; we speak of the birth of nations, artworks, stars, and now the biosphere. Unlike the strictly imaginary delivery of Bacchus from the thigh of Jupiter or of Adonis from the bark of a myrrh tree, however, reproduction of the biosphere is not just metaphor. If Earth is a physiological system with many of the attributes (thermoregulation, regulation of atmospheric oxygen composition, and so on) of a living body, then the statement that the biosphere is on the verge of reproduction partakes of biological reality.

Reproduction is accomplished with stunning variety in the natural world. It ranges from the binary fission of bacteria to the asexual mitosis of protoctists and spans across the meiotic sexual reproduction of mammals and the nuptial flight of queen bees about to begin new social insect colonies. Human beings have become necessary for the reproduction of some agricultural varieties, and many flowering plants, to reproduce, need to be eaten and disseminated by particular species of mammals and insects. Economist Kenneth Boulding once quipped, "The automobile's a species just like the horse; it just has a more complicated sex life."[1] Indeed, we might well wonder what empirically separates the proliferation of cars, which come off assembly lines due to the efforts of human autoworkers, from the reproduction of animals, which also depend upon a supportive environment. I believe there can be no such absolute empiric separation.

Animal reproduction does not, of course, depend on autoworkers, but it does depend on the reproducing plants and microbes that ply and continually resupply the biosphere with all the chemical nutrients we animals need to survive. Ultimately, the complex buildup of matter—of growth at the Earth's surface from the fracturing of an acorn into an oak tree to the production of books in a publishing house—depends on the biosphere's photosynthetic accumulation of the energy of the sun. Even dismissing the idea that machines "*self*-reproduce," it is clear that the means of reproduction in the biosphere differ radically among different kinds of organisms.

At a meeting on the need to build closed environments capable of regenerating all the supplies needed to sustain life in the extraterrestrial environment, Russell L. Schweickart complimented the emerging discipline of biospherics. A NASA astronaut from 1963 to 1979, Schweickart said:

> The grand concept of birth from planet Earth into the cosmos—in 1993, 1994, 2010, 2050, or whenever—is a calling of the highest order. I want to pay a lot of respect to everyone associated with that grand vision for their courage to move ahead with this in the face of the unknowns which make the lunar landing look like a child's play toy. There were a lot of complexities there but we were dealing with resistors, transistors, and optical systems which were very well understood. Now we're wrestling with the real question: that natural process of reproduction of this grand organism called Gaia. And that's what all the practice has been about.

Flying over the U.S. land mass one sees contrasting patches of farmland, each patch like a section of a giant quilt. From this distance one can see that the reworking of Earth begun by agriculture might intensify, be extended up and out architecturally. This development would be forced by the technological problem of pollution and the technological solution of biospherics acting together. And it would not be merely a human development but a metamorphosis of the planet as a whole. An irreversible decline in the hospitability of the terraqueous environment could force the Earth through technological humanity to differentiate into biospheric sections. As biologist Garret Hardin chronicles in an ecological essay, *Tragedy of the Commons*, the commons were collectively held lands upon which British sheep owners allowed their sheep to graze freely. But the commons did not endure; pursuing selfish advantage, sheep owners let their own animals overgraze to their own benefit but at the expense of others. The overgrazing eroded the soil until it was unable to produce enough grass for anyone's sheep. The natural phenomenon of greed had brought about the degradation of the commons. It is almost a law of ecology that, over evolutionary time, the commons become uncommon. They disappear.

Sober reflection suggests the whole surface of our planet may undergo a radical transformation, a metamorphosis of life as a whole. The Earth seems fated to turn into something like a cosmic embryo, sectioning off, fragmenting into cells, each of which will contain a version of the global ecosystem in miniature. Each differentiated section would be an enclosed ecosystem, with its own microbes, plants, and animals; its own agriculture, communication system, and economy benefiting its human inhabitants. If enough such selfish cells arise, the whole Earth may take on the appearance of a blastular entity floating and differentiating in the black amniotic fluid of space.

The difficulty is that outside such technological assemblages human metabolism could become well-nigh impossible. Although the geological development would involve the technology that assists humanity in surviving, it would nonetheless vividly recall biological reactions to threatening environments, reactions worked out by life before there was any hint of the evolution of man. A bizarre, science-fiction-like process for us, the pollution-mediated breakup of Earth into offspring biospheres would be natural and unconscious—as physiology by definition is—for Gaia or the biosphere. If industrial pollution even remotely approaches the biotechnological pollution of our microbial ancestors, humanity to survive on the surface of the Earth will have to change that surface into protective encapsulations. The technological metamorphosis stenciled above would be born of necessity, the need to provide ourselves with fresh air, drinkable water, and edible food. Discrete assemblages of organisms integrated by technology and overseen by humans would fracture our original biosphere into many smaller global ecosystems. The texture of life on Earth will have been altered forever.

As with earlier evolutionary developments, population stress would be a major culprit in restructuring the planet into sections, each with its own miniature "global" ecology. If some sweeping disease or war does not bring down our numbers, we will probably be confronted with self-poisoning of untold proportions. This will be due to our own unstifled industrial output and pollution. Like flour beetles multiplying in a bin of cereal grain at a wholesale grocery, our growth may simply be arrested by the choking effects of our own collective and diverse wastes. However, as we have seen, the "human" does not end with the eyes and fingers but continues out into the world of technological products—of fabrics, buildings, and machines. If it were simply a question of adapting to our own wastes, perhaps many of us would die and those with, say, hardy lungs resistant to smog, or those with dark skin capable of withstanding the carcinogenic, immune system–degrading effects of ultraviolet radiation from ozone depletion, would preferentially survive. Such a view overlooks the history of technology, from the agricultural overcoming of the resource base of the land to the urban and industrial surmounting of the narrow limits of agriculture. Despite their best intentions and architectural prescience, bioshelter designers actually make it possible for more people to live on Earth than ever before; they do so, again, by busting through old environmental limits with a new technology. Because of human ingenuity, it is easy to imagine our overcoming the urban lifestyle as well, bringing the ocean to each home in recycling solar algae tanks or even forming isolated systems of closed ecology within a polluted Earth.

The biospheric sections would be little biospheres not in space but on Earth. This fragmenting would actually make the Earth hardier as a whole even as it forever modified global humanity's relationship to nature. Tamed humankind, you might say. The baby earths would be born not out of some quasi-religious futurological desire to ensure life among the galaxies but from the humbler motivation of sheer necessity: without the shelter afforded by such enclaves, human beings, despite our pervasiveness on Earth (widespread species are more resistant to extinction) could become an endangered, a self-endangered, species. We are, and will continue to be, among the first to suffer the effects of our polluting activities. Burning of fossil fuels, for example, affects first of all the urban areas rife with automobile exhaust, whose carbon monoxide squelches the hope of clean, healthy air. But exhaust also contains carbon dioxide, whose atmospheric input is projected to lead to a greenhouse effect that should warm the Earth by several dangerous degrees in the next 100 years. So, too, the nitrous oxide released in fossil-fuel burning breaks down the ozone layer and perhaps plays a role in the creation of ozone holes. It is thus the very desire to save ourselves from toxic hazards that forces the biosphere to divide itself, to undergo the ecological closure without which clean air, clean water, and clean food cannot be ensured. Even without widespread pollution, the advantages of productive, resource-independent, home-sized ecological designs are increasingly becoming evident. The ecological closure inherent in forming biospheres amounts to a technological meta-morphosis of planet Earth.

Such a view of the biosphere subdivided like human property into thousands of modular regions may seem gloomy. It is a diluvian vision —not of life planning and devising biospheres to fulfill the romantic dream of sailing to the stars, but of humanity making a last-ditch effort, after much procrastination and in desperation, to procure a safe home in a globally ravaged environment. Yet the dream and the nightmare are cu-riously one. For the same imprudent biospheric technology needed as a last resort to rescue us from the fouling of the global nest is required to disseminate life as a planetary entity into outer space. Human beings have fortuitously become involved in the destiny of the Earth, as agents or midwives of its sexless reproduction.

It is claimed that a truly advanced civilization would be no more attached to the planet of its origin than a newly hatched chick is to the eggshell from which it emerges. Right now what we see are signs of the development of the unhatched Earth "egg." In some of his writings, Aristotle compared nature to art, specifically calling attention to the way an embryo acts like a "sketch" that in development is filled, just as a painter would color and complete, would "flesh out" his first tentative charcoal lines. The shape and nature of the Earth in the universe resembles an unfinished work of great beauty, ambiguity, and economy. It has direction, but its possibilities are endless. As to life's future role in the cosmos, we are still in the infancy of our understanding; nonetheless, as it takes shape this very understanding could, in some sense, and to varying degrees, help fill in the details of our fate as humans—and the ancestors, perhaps, of new species—within the history of the cosmos.

CHAPTER 14

~

Sanctuary

The pollution-mediated break-up or differentiation of the Earth into local biospheres is not a foregone conclusion; it is, rather, a fore-shortened view of the future. Similar transformations of the *oikos*, the living space, have occurred in the past as the global population rose from approximately 10 million at 10,000 years ago to over 5 billion today. The changes were mostly due to agriculture, which rendered nomadic hunting and gathering peoples obsolete. A shrunken version of the once-prevalent pastoral lifestyle—shepherds and herdsmen grazing their flocks over vast areas of grassland—came to cities as the local commons.

With the rise of agriculture and cities came private property and the fall of the commons. We still share our oceans, atmosphere, and space. But with 6 to 10 billion people projected to exist at the end of this century, what is the fate of this presently shared planetary commons? Will these Earth commons deteriorate as fast as the common lands once did? This time it will be the world ocean, atmosphere, and "near Earth" space that will have to be divided up and privatized in order to be protected from selfish overuse. Ecological closure would not be a scientific oddity, or a luxury, but the outcome of adapting to pollution. There would be no place else to live. In the future biospheres could become the three-dimensional equivalent of private property, an extension of the fences and border patrols people erect to mark the still-flat turf of their backyards and national or natural frontiers.

Overgrazing is thought to have led to the devastation of lands in India, the Middle East, and the Mediterranean and to have been a factor in the appearance and extension of deserts such as the Sahara and the Great Central Desert of Australia. Overeating of grasses erodes soil and creates dust. And, like oil, soil is the result of lengthy geological and biological processes. (Vernadsky, recall, developed his concept of the mineral nature of life from a study of soil.) Indeed, soil, due to its dependence on many living processes, may be a nonrenewable resource ultimately far more valuable than oil. The Masai, an East African tribe inhabiting Kenya and Tanzania, depend upon cattle, from whom they obtain milk—but also draw blood to drink through a vein in the neck without killing them. A symbol of wealth, large herds of cattle have replaced normal game and are now overgrazing the grasslands. Diversity is declining, and soon the former biological regime may be unrestorable. Historically, the switch to private from publicly shared property must have occurred in other populations as it is now occurring in the Masai today.

The problem of the commons is a general biological one not confined to agriculture or flat expanses of land. Commons of all kinds face the recurring problem of overuse each time a population increases. Human industrial pollution of global waterways, air supplies, and remaining reserves could be combated by centralized controls, well-thought-out and timely international treaties. But the temptation to cheat for selfish advantage doubtless will not disappear overnight. In the absence of collectivist restrictions and repressive governmental rations, the politics of private property develop as an alternative. Won't the fundamentally unresolved conflict between capitalism and communism therefore continue into space?

From a global policy or geopolitical perspective, unless very strict international accords regulating air and water pollution are enforced and effective, biospheric recyling technology will be the only way for people to ensure clean water, fresh air, and pesticide-free food. By this time the oceans may be so full of sewage, the air so rife with noxious fumes, and tap water so overloaded with lead and other pollutants that some of the most ravaged environments of today will look positively attractive by comparison. Although criticized by some as "technocratic Disneylands," and accused by others of being planned as elitist retreats for right-wing survivalists, in the long run only human-scale controlled habitats could preserve our original environment in the face of global toxic waste and pollution of the vaster commons. And this will have become not a human but a planetary or ecological phenomenon.

McHarg's Cubicle

The first Soviet efforts to build biospheres big enough to contain people were failures. What crippled early biospheres was their simplicity and smallness. They weren't ambitious *enough*. To build a biosphere humans must select the correct species. Apparently, this cannot be achieved through minimalism, but only by grafting a healthy-sized chunk of the Earth's natural diversity into a new setting.

In the 1960s Ian L. McHarg, a Scottish-born environmental architect and landsape designer from the University of Pennsylvania, pondered "how an astronaut might be sent to the moon with the least possible baggage to sustain him." The experimental environment dreamed up by McHarg consisted of a plywood capsule with a fluorescent light, air, water, algae growing in water, bacteria, and a man. With this most "modest hoard of groceries,"

[the man] consumes oxygen and exhales carbon dioxide; the algae consume carbon dioxide and expel oxygen into the air which the man breathes, and so an oxygen–carbon dioxide cycle is ensured. The man thirsts, drinks some water, urinates, this passes into the water medium in which the algae and bacteria exist, the water is consumed by the algae, transpired, condensed, the man drinks the condensations and a closed cycle of water exists. When hungry, the man eats some algae, digests them, then defecates. Subsequently, the decomposers reduce the excrement into forms utilizable by the algae, which grow. The man eats more algae, and so a food chain has been created. The only import to the system is the light from the fluorescent tube . . . the only export from the system is heat.

"Alas," concludes McHarg, "experiments of this kind have not been sustained for more than twenty-four hours, a sad commentary on our understanding of man-nature."[1]

Similarly, early versions of Soviet shelters, part of the "Bios" series, were claustrophobic, as small as twelve cubic meters. One unsuccessful early Soviet model even contained a minimalist system similar to the one described by McHarg: but *Chlorella*—a hardy, protein-rich unicellular alga used to purify the water and air—gave off too much oxygen and proved to be less effective than plants at cleaning the air. Nor did *Chlorella*, which tastes terrible, epitomize *haute cuisine* or provide a quality source of nutrition. In general, the setup was not overly conducive to either human physical or mental health.

To make functioning biospheres, the food cycle cannot be cut as short as it was in this early model. As in the larger biosphere, which we human beings endanger by our tendency to simplify ecosystems—to cut out intermediary species and channel all food and resources directly to ourselves—this conscious effort to economize on a small scale backfired. To eliminate "superfluous" producers and consumers from their natural habitat—to move straight from algal photosynthesizer to human omnivore (as envisioned in McHarg's oversimplification)—is—either on the great scale of the Earth or in the tiny setting of a life-support system—to court environmental disaster.

The Bios Project

On November 11, 1983, two Siberian engineers, Nikolai Bugreyev and Sergei Alexeyev, entered Bios 3, the third Soviet version of a completely enclosed cosmonaut capsule.[2] While provisioned with only one month's supply of food and separated from civilization except for electricity and television, the two researchers survived the Siberian winter, emerging from the enclosure's Earth-bound hull some five months after the metal door had been shut. More recent models in the Bios program are nearly the size of Skylab and contain up to thirteen square meters of planted area per researcher, with dill, peas, wheat, kohlrabi (a cabbage derivative), and many other vegetables growing under xenon lamps, whose spectral light-emission properties are similar to those of the sun. Bypassing the soil, the vegetables grow directly in specially prepared, nutrient-rich water. The stated purpose of the Soviet Bios projects is to reproduce on an interplanetary ship all the pertinent biology that occurs on Earth. A spacecraft or community in orbit can be continually resupplied by cargo ships, but soaring (or diving) away from Earth requires freedom from merely "camping out" in space. Biospherics, the technology of ecology, is required for long-term space travel and to sever the rocket-fuel umbilical cord to Mama EarthSky.

Soviet and NASA scientists agree that missions of people to Mars or beyond—perhaps with citizens of two or more nations going together to the vicarious thrill of us all—would require the application not only of astronautics but of biospherics. In "astrobiospherics" inner and outer space merge, and we realize that wherever we hang our biospheric hat, that is our home.

The Schoolroom

We have already encountered ecospheres, desk-top marine ecosystems in the form of crystal balls; the ecospheres do for Hawaiian fairy shrimp what McHarg contemplated and the Soviets attempted doing with humans. Although too small for mammals, ecospheres are living lessons in interdependence, in how life works in a circumscribed space, with limited, necessarily recycling bioresources. Held up in a child's hands, they remind us of more than the science-fiction dream of dwelling in space, of the wholly natural recycling technologies needed to free extraterrestrial inhabitants from the continuous need to ferry supplies up from Earth.

Beyond and before this, ecospheres epitomize the type of ecological harmony needed by us on the outside. If a schoolgirl can see that too much sunlight can quickly kill all but one shrimp, she can imagine what effect destruction of the ozone layer—which lets in a rain of ultraviolet light—would have on *our* biosphere. If children are exposed to and encouraged to play with such spheres in grade school or before, perhaps the next generation will have a more realistic idea of what mutual survival entails. Usually remote and theoretical problems such as acid rain, the greenhouse effect, and water pollution come home and crystallize in such a circumscribed locus. These ecological worries become almost palpable when a miniaturized ecological world is put on a tabletop. Life is seen as a complex knot, the necessity of its "econnections" as obvious as the laces of a well-tied shoe. If every classroom on Earth had an ecosphere next to its national flag and biologically inaccurate colorful globe full of national divisions not seen from space, perhaps the notion would dawn that the fundamental unit of our life is not the individual human being or tribe or nation but includes the entire community of organisms supporting us—a community from which children in cities the world over have of late become increasingly estranged.

The threat we now pose to ourselves has made it imperative for national boundaries to begin to be minimized and for planetary humanity to ally itself to the Gaian ecosystem operating above and beyond all national frontiers. The prime enemy facing us is no longer as obvious as the military powers of any one nation (despite Soviet and U.S. nuclear arsenals). It is rather the far more subtle but steadily encroaching collapse of the biological regime upon which we as humans depend. We must band together to fight an enemy, but this enemy is not political; nor does it consist of human beings or any other species. The prime enemy now is the ecological ignorance of the Earth as a single physiological system that will not put up with insults. If Gaia exists, she is, as Lovelock says, no doting English nanny but an organized, self-sustaining system that will react with all the warmth and sympathy of an electronic circuit in the microbrain of an intercontinental ballistic missile. What threatens us now threatens all of us. It is the generalized enemy of ignorance coming from no specific corner. To ensure our mutual survival we must band together, study the Earth as a single system, and be wary of the ecological complacency which suggests that, just because we have survived so far by behaving in a certain way toward the biosphere, such behavior can continue indefinitely in the same way it always has.

Reproductive Representation

Biospheres remain unborn. Only with the production of controlled living systems—only with the experience of dividing or having divided from her self—will nature lose her primordial inchoate innocence. As test-tube microcosms, ecospheres, and the Bios projects attest, the biosphere is coming out of itself, as if from a dream. Beside itself, the biosphere gains the capacity for *physical* self-reflexivity. And in this alienation, which is division, nature's cosmic perpetuation becomes infinitely assured.

Becoming isolated from herself, Gaia through us, will experience all the joys of motherhood; yet in another sense, the entire surface of the

Earth could divide into smaller global physiological sections and nature still will not have reproduced. For growth is not reproduction. The strange economy of nature is such that she is already always divided from herself and yet unified at the same time. Reproduction of some beings are necessary for the self-preserving maintenance of others. Humanity reproduces on the surface of the Earth to the point of extreme danger. But then, through technology, we begin to behave like the tiny cellular spots that draw the genetic material apart during the process of cell division. As nature divides from herself she comes to see herself as different. She compares herself to herself. And this dividing, this moving away to observe, further divides and further requires new observation. The self-examining project of nature epitomized by representation and reproduction remains so urgent because it is forever incapable of being finished.

Biosphere II

In the United States a group of venture capital and ecological management firms is undertaking the construction of an artificial world— "Biosphere II," a prototype of a controlled world not unlike those that eventually might catapult humans into space or provide sanctuary in a ravaged earthly home. But Biosphere II could also be a "laboratory," concretely demonstrating the principles of a fledgling "ecosophy" (a coinage from the Greek meaning "home wisdom"): it could serve as a "control" world where the possibly disastrous planetary effects of our actions could be modeled before they reach a crisis stage. The vivid project of a self-sustaining human habitat on Earth—an ecosphere for people rather than for shrimp—could become an important example and message for the peoples of the Earth. It might even induce us to take the actions necessary to prevent biospheres from becoming more than a scientific curiosity. In other words, the implication that we are going to live in sealed glass cages could scare people and nations into a new ecological harmony with the Earth that will prevent this from being the case.

Presently under construction on a 2300-acre (930-hectare) ranch north of the Santa Catalina Mountains near Tucson, Arizona, Biosphere II will appear on land once owned by the Countess of Suffolk, an American widowed by her British husband. The land, bought by the Motorola Corporation, was used as a conference center but then was donated to the University of Arizona. The University of Arizona sold it to Space Biospheres Ventures for approximately 3.4 million U.S. dollars. Currently known as SunSpace Ranch, this area is a sort of scientific oasis in the middle of the desert—as biospheres on Mars would have to be also. From the outside you would not expect that the architecture completed so far, reminiscent of native and early American culture, contains tissue culture laboratories and precision scientific apparatus necessary to construct and monitor what may well be the world's largest enclosed terraquarium. If successful, the sealed metal-and-glass structure will be a testing ground of environmental theories, enhancing our knowledge of biogeochemical cycles, acid rain, soil erosion, waste processing, and weather.

Already built is a test module of Biosphere II. Roughly 18,000 cubic feet (500 cubic meters), the test module has been designed to test the materials, glazing techniques, computer-controlled louvers (windows that can let different amounts of light into different areas of the structure), and solar heating and cooling systems. It must be ascertained, for example, that dangerous volatiles used in construction do not slip away to poison the life inside the biosphere. The test module also tests a special "lung" that expands and contracts due to the sealing of the structure and therefore its exposure to potentially catastrophic changes in atmospheric pressure. The "lung" exemplifies the sort of organic architecture necessary in this building, which is at the same time the outside of a living structure. Able to inflate or deflate in response to barometric pressure changes, the lung can save the glass or seal from cracking. Phillip Hawes, co-architect of Biosphere II and one-time student of both Bruce Goff and Frank Lloyd Wright, recalls architecture classes in which a student handed in a design for a house located in a floating zeppelin. He notes that simply to seal something as big as Biosphere II represents a huge advance in biospheric technology.

The test module, although only 0.3 percent the finished volume of Biosphere II, is still, as far as I know, the largest sealed structure that admits light. Biosphere II when finished will be as long at points as 540 feet (165 meters), and as wide, in some places, as 340 feet (104 meters).

Also near the site of Biosphere II stands a greenhouse-aquaculture-tissue culture laboratory. The complex serves as a support structure to Biosphere II in which techniques of propagation, cultivation, and species selection for Biosphere II, production/biomass yields, and maximum re-cycling short of actual material closure can be studied. In the tissue culture laboratory plants are cloned in a microbe-free environment by carefully separating starter cells under the microscope. The plants grown from the starter cells are sold locally to nurseries, and the money generated is channeled back into the Biosphere II project.

The laboratory's director, horticulturist Stephen Storm, is perfecting a technique for cloning the neem tree, a native plant of central India that contains azadirachtin, a natural insecticide. Beetles, which feed on other insects, also look promising as a form of nontoxic pest control within a very circumscribed community. The cycles of foods into waste and pollutants into the environment are so much more rapid in an enclosed habitat that it would potentially be fatal to use chemical pesticides in a cavalier fashion. Whereas pesticides may spread throughout the planetary ecosystem within a century, pesticides sprayed in the morning in a biosphere would be on dinner plates by evening. Even innocuous chemicals such as antibiotics and vegetable hormones (including ethylene, which makes tomatoes ripen or prematurely rot) must be carefully watched inside biospheres so they don't wreak havoc. According to Carl Hodges, the chief environmental engineer on the project (and a main designer of the Land Pavilion, the history-of-agriculture exhibit at Disney's Epcot Center), the stream running through the middle of Biosphere II will be "the most analyzed stream in the world." This indoor stream will fill from "rain" on the ceiling, moving condensed precipitation from the structure's "atmosphere" down to its miniature marsh, desert, rainforest, savanna, and "ocean" ecosystems, complete with coral reefs.

Over 5 million cubic feet, spanning acres, Biosphere II has been billed by its makers as the "most valuable piece of real estate in the world" and the "most exciting scientific project going on on the planet."[3] During the 1990s several "biospherians" are slated to enter the structure, with the goal of living inside for two years. Already biologist Abigale Alling has survived for five days (March 3–13, 1989) within the test module, a steel-framed greenhome with a twenty-foot ceiling over a twenty-three-square-foot base. The test module—the size of a two-story house compared with Biosphere II's two and one-half acres—provided 29-year-old Alling with 2500 calories a day from twenty-nine plant species, including carrots, potatos, beans, papaya, and strawberries. Entering the enclosure clad in a red jumpsuit, the Yale University–trained biologist commented, "I will live, move, and breathe in another life system. . . . it is another world, and a world apart from where you are. It is a remarkable feat."[4] The ultimate goal is to create biospheres that can support human beings permanently, indefinitely.

Those left shut inside biospheric structures when their airlocks are sealed underscore pollution problems for the rest of us. As Carl Hodges put it, the biospherians

> will know as they take a deep breath that that breath would not be possible unless the green plants around them are fixing carbon and providing them with oxygen. They will know that the molecules that make up the water that rains from the ceiling of Biosphere II will at one time be part of the carbohydrates that provide them with their energy. And they will know that the contamination of that water by any foolish activity on their part will poison their biosphere and therefore themselves.

Hodges, whose Environmental Research Laboratory specializes in hydroponics (plants grown without soil in water), halophytes (plants irrigated with salt water), and solar design as well as biospherics, advocates pure food that can be grown in closed systems. His salad vegetables, fortified by nitrates from algae and fish waste in the same tanks, and tilapia, a delicious species of fish reared in Egyptian ponds for thousands of years, will be staples of the biospherian diet.

The biospherians of Biosphere II will be connected to the outside world with telephone, telex, television, radio, video, computer networks, and telefax. They will maintain a computer "hotline" to experts in charge of each ecosystem type of biome, experts such as Amazon biologist Ghillean Prance, senior vice president of the New York Botanical Garden in charge of the jungle ecosystem, and Walter Adey, director of the Smithsonian Institution's Marine Systems Laboratory, in charge of Biosphere II's miniature ocean and marsh systems. Whether humanity can really measure up to the demands of global environmental responsibility will be put to a test here. And the ecological "dramatization" could be crucial both for politics and science—or, rather, for politics as science. By playing with it, Biosphere II can be exposed to environmental problems—geophysiological ailments—that may already be afflicting "Biosphere I"— the body of the Earth. The "greenhouse effect" brought about by the burning of fossil fuels and thus an increasing insulating blanket of transparent carbon dioxide in our atmosphere, could make icy Greenland

green, put New York City under water, and make the midwest a desert
by 2040. In trial runs with the test module, carbon dioxide was roughly
five times higher in the biosphere than on Earth. In Biosphere II carbon
dioxide levels may be elevated even further to simulate the greenhouse
effect. By shutting down the computer-monitored louvers of Biosphere
II, the effect of an absence of light thought to occur in a nuclear winter
during the aftermath of nuclear war could be inspected. (The devastating
effects of nuclear winter also depend on a lowering of temperature that
might, in the Arizona desert, prove more difficult to simulate.) The good
news is that such experiments will focus public attention on biotic interdependence, on symbiotic econnections in the broadest sense of the term.
The makers of Biosphere II have every hope that the presence of their
structure will raise ecological consciousness to a new level.

Former astronaut Joseph Allen, who spoke at Biospheres Conference
II, convened by the Institute of Ecotechnics in September, 1985, suggests
that the science of comparing biospheres may become as important to our
understanding of the biological world as is modern quantum mechanics
to a grasp of the physical world. Allen, both astronaut and physicist, points
out that the insights of quantum mechanics were due in part to Niels
Bohr's mathematical synthesis and comparison of the nuclear antics of
hydrogen and helium atoms. Think of the importance for modern science
of exploring other planets, so-called "comparative planetology." The in-
terdisciplinary study relating Earth to other bodies in our solar system
became possible only with the accumulation of information gained by
orbiting and landing down upon our planetary neighbors. The chemical
disequilibrium of the Earth's atmosphere suggests that the Earth "is alive"
only in the new context of the relative "deadness" of our planetary neighbors Mars and Venus. Bearing in mind the importance of these studies
of other planets, what might the existence of other *living* worlds tell us?
Creating a Biosphere II (or III or IV) may prove to be a scientific gold
mine. Creating other living worlds is destined not only to enrich our
science but to shift the whole foundations of our emerging planetary
consciousness. As with one eye there is no perception of depth, so with
one biosphere our view of the universe lacks depth. A multiplicity of
biospheres not only creates specific new angles of vision; it multiplies
perspectives. It may also produce a whole new *kind* of vision, a sort of
biological "hyperspective." The Earth becomes a cosmic eye without a
body; with each new biosphere that is produced, this eye grows more

compound, like the eye of an insect. Metaphorically, the compound eye of a biospheric Earth could come to see the entire universe as its extensive body, a body whose parts are too heavy or distant to move. Speechless, we witness the endless pupal metamorphosis of our own body, powerless to do anything but watch.

A Second Nature

Whether or not Biosphere II as an American project succeeds or fails is secondary. What is foremost is that those who live in new biospheres —whether on Earth, on a space voyage, in a Martian settlement, or beyond—inhabit a sort of second nature. The experience of self-reliance within such a second nature recalls the experience of Henry David Thoreau. A nineteenth-century naturalist, Thoreau lived out his philosophy —or ecosophy—of self-reliance in Concord, Massachusetts, at Walden Pond. I have gone there, skipping stones across the surface of the water, watching the rings spread silently at sunset—before being disturbed, as Thoreau never was, by AM radios and noisy planes flying overhead. I mention this because the meditative experience of entering an extraterrestrial biosphere can never again be done without being surrounded by technology as well. Architect Paolo Soleri remarked that the first requirement of moving into space is that we be "intentionally naïve." Here, at the start of commercial biosphere production, part of our naïveté may be that the technological production of living miniatures of the Earth is so spanking new. But even later we will not know it all. Do a man and woman have to know the anatomy of the reproductive system in order to make a baby? On a cognitive level, of course not, but on an unconscious, subliminal level, their bodies do.

The same applies to biosphere production. Building a living system beyond Earth requires knowledge, but the knowledge is still only partial, more a knowledge of how than why. Architects can go to senior architects or study the works of the old masters. But where is the blueprint of the Earth? The divine vault remains closed and so biospheric architects must replace precedent with intuition and instinct. Engineering and equations, nuts and bolts are necessary to construct a house but are not sufficient to create a new living world. "Without life," Vernadsky wrote, "the face of the Earth would become as motionless and inert as the face of the moon."

The flowing water in which life arose moves beyond water but still retains the flowing principle of the wave. If one stares at a waterfall for several minutes, and then looks away to the cliff that surrounds it, the solid rocks will seem to rush upward like a fluid. Indeed, the hard parts of life are, over geological time, malleable and fluid. The Earth is not stagnant and still like the cratered surface of Mars or the moon. It turns over. It rocks and rolls. Instead of craters it has lakes, lakes that fill with rain produced by the chemical operations of life. The aqueous and metamorphosing surfaces of this planet are also a technology, but a technology as elegant as the blood and bones of the human body, whose inner workings, so amazingly run, depend not at all on our conscious understanding. Thus there is a wisdom in nature, an elusive ecosophy that we can approach but never subsume.

I don't think Thoreau would be a stranger to the comment that our bodies, our senses, are fashioned by the same creative forces of which they make use. This alluring reflexivity has no final interpretation, only ever more beautiful ones. All human art is nature's art put through a self-hiding, self-disclosing mask, a mask of nature's modesty with herself and that which she has not yet become. This mask has two sides. One side is time; the other side is incarnation, matter:

> What is man but a mass of thawing clay? The ball of the human finger is but a drop congealed . . . is not the hand a spreading *palm* leaf with its lobes and veins? The ear may be regarded, fancifully, as a lichen, *umbilicaria*, on the side of the head, with its lobe or drop. The lip—labium, from *labor*—laps or lapses from the sides of the cavernous mouth. The nose is a manifest congealed drop or stalactite.[5]

This is what Thoreau saw in the hour of his tour, in the season of his introspective walks around Walden Pond. In this season he participated directly with the evidence of nature; his gaze was unfiltered by the cheese-cloth of received wisdom. Not avoiding contingency but evading at least conventional cliches, Thoreau plunged himself into the maze of nature and described biological details in a way uncensored by public opinion or scientific peer review. Though perhaps more locally than globally, and with a sensibility informed more by nature walks and observation than scientific speculation, Thoreau perceived like Vernadsky: he not only communicated but communed with nature; he watched it mutely, in serene rapture; he felt it as a (w)hole.

In retrospect, however, perhaps Thoreau, in his love for the wild, for the fertile swamps and forest details, missed the Butlerian train of thought that the steam engines rattling through the woods were also mineral deposits in motion, transformations of earthly metallic veins and giant fern forests into black coal and the rhythmic trudging of iron. The veins begin as bands of ore buried in the Earth and grow into railroad tracks branching across continents. Technology is not a wrong track but an extension of nature's ancient creativity so sudden it startles us. We may protest against the tackiness of technology, its inelegance and obtrusiveness, but this clumsiness is a mark of its newness, like the uncoordinated gait of a newly born fawn. As we watch the baby deer of technology stumble through these springtime woodlands it is easy to be condescending. What we forget is that the fawn is already walking, just hours after she has been born. If we look closely we can see in this very ungainliness of youth the promise of a future elegance, an elegance in which "our" technology has come into harmony with nature. This then is the fate of technology: to leave behind the immature stages of antagonism and courtship and to permanently mate or copulate with the biospheric life from which it has sprung.

CHAPTER 15

~

Dissemination

Reproducing biospheres represent a new hour in the human day, a new age in the Earth's ontogeny. If we could examine history under the temporal equivalent of a microscope, we might be startled by the resemblance to organisms and cells of biospheres. Biospheres are emblematic of the elusive property of individuality. It is a property we attribute not only to ourselves, multicelled organisms, but also to animals and swimming microorganisms. Many organisms and collections have reproduced before. Many have stopped growth temporarily to form resistant structures protecting them until better times. Biospheres themselves, technological though they may be, strikingly resemble Earth's seeds. Even the simplest organisms on Earth deal with hardship by forming propagules. Propagules, hard and durable, resist death from drying out from solar radiation. They encase, encapsulate, and protect. They propagate. The biospheric production of biospheres is like the seed formation of a flowering plant before it scatters its seeds far and wide. It is propagation by, of, and for the Earth, *through* humanity. Biospheres are not human property but are only entrusted to us temporarily. Properly speaking, they belong to the Earth. In a graph of the geological history of the Earth, humanity would appear as a mere glich. Biospheres, however, would be marked off, highlighted, or underlined. They stand out. They are not another animal species but the reappearance of individuality on an immense scale, achieving dimensions not yet seen during the course of biological evolution. Biospheres are the flesh and blood of the Earth. They are its own.

To understand the assertion that biosphere formation recapitulates ancient means of organic survival, let us consider some examples more pedestrian than the Earth as a living whole. The endospores of the bacterium *Clostridium* are propagules. So are the seeds of plants and eggs of animals. Hibernating in caves is the propagule-like behavior engaged in by some bear species. The tardigrade or "water bear," a pond invertebrate that through a scanning electron microscope looks amazingly like a bear, exemplifies the effectiveness of propagule strategies. When food becomes scarce, or when a tardigrade incurs bodily damage, it forms a "cyst," a thick-walled enclosure in which the animal contracts and its organs deteriorate. Yet the tardigrade is not dead; it can regenerate to live again. Tardigrades also periodically dry out, metamorphosing into immobile, barrel-shaped forms called "tuns"—the name for wine casks, which describes what they look like. As tuns, water bears can survive a very long time—some people say 100 years. In their various protective enclosures, tardigrades can withstand temperatures ranging from 151° to − 270° C (a temperature that freezes into liquids atmospheric gases such as nitrogen and oxygen). And they can tolerate an X-ray dose of 570,000 roentgens (which would kill a person a thousand times over). Not surprisingly, considering their ability to form propagules, tardigrade species inhabit both the arctic and the tropic zones, as well as places in between.

But do not human enclosures—our cars and apartment buildings, our airplanes and schools—also partake of this ancient process of protecting the soft and vulnerable within ever harder and more durable settings? Are not modern houses, with central heating and air conditioning, *already* well on the way toward the separated biospheric enclosures of the future? In a way, our bodies themselves are simply a strange agglomeration or concatenation of Earth that has lifted up, come loose from gravity. This most simple and marvelous example of people walking (which I owe to Eugene Mallove)—in effect represents the Earth coming detached from itself and mobile. We *are* the Earth biomineralizing. By forming plants and animals and human beings the Earth is *already* differentiating into discrete sections. Once again, we need not wait for some science-fiction future to be amazed. Futuristic technology is, already, always, here.

Insectophilia

Insects are not particularly prized by our culture and we tend to dismiss as creepy crawlers anything resembling a bug. Because insects are by far the most numerous class of animals on Earth, one suspects that our fear and disgust with insects owes by and large to our having to compete with them. For starters, there can be no doubt that from a survival standpoint insects are extremely successful, variations of a design that have proven by and large far more fruitful than that of the sparse oversized mammals. When asked if he had learned anything about God from his biological studies, biologist J.B.S. Haldane replied, "an inordinate fondness for beetles." Judged by the number of catalogued species, beetles are extraordinarily prolific, the most successful form of animal life on Earth.

Haldane's quip about the deity's taste seems also to apply to the ancient Egyptians. For, of the many things (including time and language) that separate our culture from that of the ancient Egyptians, an attitude toward insects is certainly one. Just as the English are considered mycophobic (afraid of mushrooms) while eastern European peoples are considered mycophilic (fond of mushrooms), so the ancient Egyptians appear to have been "insectophilic" rather than, like us, "insectophobic." That is, they may not have simply disliked insects as annoying bugs, but rather feared and respected them for their metamorphoses and transformations, for their astounding ability to propagate.

Part of the remarkable survival powers—and not only of the class *Insecta* but of the whole phylum of arthropods—can be traced to the making of exoskeletons—to the covering of their *outsides* in hard, structurally supportive materials. From cockroaches and lice to ladybug beetles and lobsters (the first two are particularly irksome because they live off the human habitat), arthropods are protected in the hard biogenic coating called chitin. The only equivalent in mammals is the relatively unimpressive keratin, a hard protein that forms hair and horns and nails but which does not enclose the entire body. Our clothes and cars and houses, all our dwellings in the glorified burrow-lands we call the modern city, perhaps come closer to the propagule-like strategy of forming a hard exterior. These similarities to insects, of course, have been unconscious on our part. However, this may not have been the case with the ancient Egyptians. Ironically, from our ethnocentric point of view, the purpose of the great Egyptian pyramids may have been to erect durable protective structures *precisely like* those that come naturally and are the birthright of dung or scarab beetles. By emulating the insect life cycle, the Pharaohs prepared themselves for a metamorphosis into the afterlife.

The Pharaohs who had themselves mummified and buried in caverns at the bases of giant pyramids seem mystifyingly idiosyncratic to us today. In their own frame of reference, however, the ancient Egyptians probably thought themselves eminently practical. In piling up great triangular configurations of limestone over their recumbent and swathed bodies, their leaders were simply copying the behavior of the dung beetle (family Scarabaeidae), a ground-burrowing insect the Egyptians worshipped, following its complex life in a double sense, and attributing to the being a mythological significance. The wearing of scarabs, made either of the dried exoskeletons or of other materials in the shape of scarab beetles, around the neck as jewelry or pendants is a vestige of this worship.

Dung beetles roll balls of dung in which to lay eggs and on which the larvae feed. Egyptians employed as a talisman and symbol of resurrection the form of this beetle, carved either in stone or in earthenware decorated with opaque, colored glazes (faïence). According to old Egyptian folklore, the male beetle wishing to procreate found a piece of ox dung. The sacred beetle shaped the piece of ox dung into a ball with his hind legs, rolling it from east to west, then buried the ball in a special hole dug out for this purpose and left it there for twenty-eight days. On the twenty-ninth day the beetle pushed the dung into water in order for its young to emerge.

In the ancient Egyptian religion there was a correspondence between the ball of dung, rolled in the life-storing process of propagation from east to west, and the sun, which also gave life and moved from east to west. Moreover, recent scholarship suggests that, by descending after death to the Earth with all their possessions, the Pharaohs were attempting to preserve themselves as hard parts in preparation for a journey into a new form. After all, if an insect can live long by transforming from one sort of body to another, what prevents human beings from considering their old age and death as illusory—a prelude to a grander life to come, a blossoming into another sort of body or phase of being? An examination of the natural history of insects, particularly scarab beetles, may have seduced those ancient dwellers of the Nile that their fates—properly decked out with food and supplies for the interim voyage—could prove likewise. As a beetle prepares for the new life of its young by covering itself with earth, so the Pharaohs buried their material remains beneath a momentous agglomeration of rock. Suddenly the Egyptian religion seems almost biospheric, deeply in tune with life's use of mineral forms, its protective encapsulation in bodies and propagules.

The Other Side of Time

However unsuccessful the Pharaohs may have been, now the Earth itself seems to be opting for a form of propagule formation. The biosphere is "adopting" these strategies, not so much out of conscious design as out of the incessant evolution of the beings within it. This fairly hieroglyphic process is latent within the structure of the Earth. Propagule formation, the "seeding" of the biosphere prior to its dissemination, is as natural as a larval metamorphosis, the shedding of old hard parts in preparation for a new life. Language, technology, humanity, physicality, meaning—all of these are included latently and blatantly in the workings of the Earth, in the global regime. Each successful encapsulation of Earth life in the technological extrastructure of a biosphere represents an Earth "seed"— part of a pod-forming or blossoming process that is more central to life than are plants, fungi, or animals. By forming biospheres, Earth enters a stage of propagule formation preparatory to dissemination and cosmic metamorphosis. In such a dissemination and metamorphosis it becomes clear that technology was never anything but natural.

This latest exquisite twist in the spiral of being affords us sudden insight into our past. The twist is a turning into the "technological spring." Entering this turning we find that "our" past is not our past so much as a past shared with life as a whole—though civilization has forgotten this in the continuing isolation of its agricultural, industrial, and technological phases.

We find that we belong inside a living world, an incalculable maze of responsive entities, all subtly impinging on us. Biospheric regulation, at a physiochemical level that can never be separated from our emotional and mental lives, represents a new explanatory principle, a new way to understand. Like all great systems of thought, this explanatory principle even hints at why we don't understand—because we are engulfed in a living thing literally outside of and containing our comprehension.

In another sense, the explanatory principle is not really new, for the idea that the Earth is alive belonged among the deepest beliefs of our ancestors. Nor, strictly speaking, is the biosphere a new form of life. Because the biosphere has maintained itself in a dynamic equilibrium for almost one-third the age of the universe, it is difficult to argue that it has just awoken (through the achievement of a critical living mass) from some inanimate slumber. Rather, it has been alive for eons. The new form of life is not the biosphere but *biospheres*, its miniaturized offspring. The new form of life represents only secondarily a human renaissance. Primarily it is the rebirth of the Earth itself, the breaking up of the Earth into earths. If the Earth is looked at as a flower, then the formation of ecospheres, biospheres, and other self-sustaining communities represents the putting to seed of this flower. The seeds are propagating but have not yet been disseminated. Space still looks too cold to dive into. In the chronically subjective sense of time that waits for us beyond the orbit of this planet it is not even May. What time is it? It is no time. Spring is still coming.

Folsomes's flasks, ecospheres, New Alchemy and Ocean Ark designs, Soviet Bios projects, and Biosphere II represent the first buds and blossoms of a cosmic springtime in which the Earth itself will bloom into the space between the stars, copying itself over in miniature, descending through the heavens, as Darwin might put it, with modification. Several points must be made about this process that seems at first so dependent upon our skills and motivations as technological humans. The first point is that biospherically humanity is not only dispensable to the metabolism of the Earth but to its reproduction as well. Only the timetable of biosphere reproduction would be upset by the absence of humanity. In the absence of humanity other organisms would evolve or re-evolve technological prowess. The fossil record reveals increasing cranial capacity in a wide range of organisms, especially the mammals. The augmentation of neural networks identified as the cause of the increased intelligence is widespread, not solely a human phenomenon. Humanity is thus not the last word but an index of increasing planetary complexity and global intelligence. Evolutionarily, intelligence is expanding. In the absence of people, many species that are ecologically repressed by our activities would be free to expand into new territories. Squirrels, monkeys, raccoons all come to mind as animals with the potential over evolutionary time to redevelop technology. Their descendants could even discover in the future fossil record our technological detritus, which might allow them to retrace our steps or make shortcuts in the task of technological advancement. The idea of a squirrel or a raccoon sitting at a computer keyboard sounds absurd; however, we are not talking about these relatively dextrous animals but about their descendants, whom they need resemble only remotely. In retrospect, science-fiction writers realize they have often erred in making predictions that were not bold enough. The destiny of technology as a planetary rather than human matter, in the hands (or grippers) of whatever species, may belong to this category, realistic to the extent it sounds absurd. Any brainy technological animal would develop tribes and civilizations and, due to overcrowding on Earth that would eventually develop, would be forced along the same opening paths that presently are bringing us as humans to the brink of biosphere formation and geogenesis.

Ultimately we are not required to enable the cosmic spread of planetary life. From a biospheric viewpoint, humanity must be considered not transcendent but only transient. We, too, will pass. Into what we do not know. Now we occupy center stage, the very thick of things. Tomorrow, who knows? We will most likely be gone, or so mutated into remnants, traces of our former selves, that we would not recognize our very progeny. One cannot say that humankind is not a special species. We are. But we are not that special. As in space, the human form, should it endure at all, will evolve, and be pantropically transformed beyond recognition. The whole history of the human race could be erased, appearing only as traces in forms of future life that defy the imagination, except insofar as we may predict the existence of some sort of structural unity on the level not of multicelled organisms but of multiorganism biospheres, recycling biosystems taking after the Earth.

Even on Earth the possibility of a pollution-mediated breakup of the planetary ecosystem into independent ecological islands—each a sort of zoo kept by the human beings it contains—raises questions about future life. What will life be like in a biosphere? Either in space or on Earth the biospheric metamorphosis has fearful connotations for humankind; it suggests a new isolation and alienation, a claustrophobia of geographic dimensions. At the same time, the geographical isolation occurring in the wake of offspring biosphere formation could allow for independent evolution, a radiation of new forms of animal life more dramatic, by far, than any that has occurred on Earth till now. Geographic isolation is the phenomenon of genetic ostracism. It permitted, for example, the marsupial bloom—the evolution on the isolated continent of Australia of those curious mammals with maternal pouches such as the kangaroo and koala bear. The differences between marsupials and placental mammals provide a clue to the type of diverging directions evolutionary development can take when ancestral populations are divided. What sort of creatures would arise inside genetically isolated, geographically withdrawn biospheres? In biospheres organisms would be reproductively isolated, species would be prevented from interbreeding, and consequently new varieties of life would evolve. On other planets, biospheres would act as a sort of settling propagule to establish an Earthlike environment. Once an Earthlike environment is established, however, local conditions—such as the dryness and cold of the red planet Mars, or the chemically reduced frozen gases and Saturnian tug of Titan—might begin to impinge themselves upon emigrant life forms. In space, many species will change radically away from their ancestral Earth forms, the familiar species of plants, animals, and fungi as we know them today. Combined with technology and the organizing modular principle of biospheres, the pace of evolutionary development in space may well exceed that of human inventions and technological development on Earth. And this applies whether or not human beings remain the predominant force within biospheres and the biospheric process of greening the universe.

On Earth or in space, communication between and among biospheres would be advantageous and would present biospherians not only with new technological challenges but also with the possibility of achieving major technological breakthroughs. If communication between neurons (nerve cells in the brain) is the physiological basis of mind, what might accrue from the cosmic intermingling of biospheres? In chemical and electromagnetic communication separately performing biospheres might ally to become the basis of still larger and more complex life forms. These, in turn, might provide the basis for a cosmos which is, not only in limited parts, but through and through, alive. Moreover, this very possibility suggests that the principle of a totally living universe is not foreign to the nature of the universe but may, rather, be part of its essence. Man, that is, may represent the groggy arising or coming-to-self of a universe already always, in its slumbering or conscious totality, alive.

On an ecologically ravaged Earth, or in sterile interstellar space, what will it be like outside the protective envelope of biospheres? Will the new outside of life be as important in the intellectual development of future beings as gap junctions and synapses are thought to be in the thinking of the human brain?

Here I might only speculate loosely about the possibility of a future cosmic mind. Even broaching such topics recalls philosophies such as Gottfried Wilhelm von Leibniz's concept of the universe as the mind of God. Much theoretical science these days is the fulfilling, in a largely secular culture, of longings once confined to the religious realm. In one sense it is highly artificial to think about the future, either science fiction (futurological) or religious (eschatological), because the future, in an important philosophical-linguistic sense, does not exist. There is no history, evolutionary or otherwise, nor future, science fiction or otherwise, but only always the language-filled present. Linguistic convention creates the illusion of time's arrow; life is, before and after all, (only) a sign. We are steeped in the medium we discuss.

The idea of the eternal present outside of time's would-be flow allows us to formulate other biospheric concepts. For the idea suggests that the future garden that the cosmos is postulated to become in one sense already is. The future and the past are already here in this line of type, this paper-thin sliver of the Earth spread between your hands. Although numerous philosophers and peoples could now be cited, let us take, more or less at random, the comments of German philosopher and co-inventor (along with Isaac Newton) of calculus, Gottfried Leibniz.

Leibniz saw the universe as an infinitely detailed image of itself. He was encouraged by his mathematical successes, once defining a straight line as "a curve, any part of which is similar to the whole, and it alone has this property, not only among curves but among sets."[1] He believed that minute portions of the world are as precisely organized and as complex as large portions, and that the "*connection* of all created things with every single one of them and their adaptation to every single one, as well as the connection and adaptation of every single thing to all others, has the result that every single substance stands in relations which express all the others. Whence every single substance is a perpetual living mirror of the universe."[2] A more up-to-date formulation of this microcosmic view of a correspondence between the individual "I" and the universal "all" can be found in many of the writings of physicist David Bohm, who, in trying to find the common ground between relativity theory and quantum mechanics, has proposed that a person is in some sense a microcosm of the universe; therefore what we are is a clue to what the universe is. Human beings are not isolated from but are enfolded with the fabric of the universe. In Bohm's notion of the implicate order—that everything is enfolded within, or *implies*, everything else—the totality of existence is enfolded within each region of space and time. Although the universe may come unstitched, each part of it is like a seed that can, properly sown, give rise to the whole. "Everything implicates everything in an order of undivided wholeness." One of Bohm's favorite examples of this idea is a transparent container full of very viscous fluid such as molasses in which ink is dropped and stirred very slowly. If you watch ink stirred this way it unwinds into a grey thread. But if the stirrer is reversed, the droplet is reconstituted— it becomes "explicate," in Bohm's language. In Bohm's view each part of the universe, each person,, is altered, jumbled, enfolded—scrambled like the grey thread. And yet preserved in each one of us are traces of the unity of the whole—past, present, and future. [3]

In 1922 George Perrigo Conger submitted a thin book in partial fulfillment for the requirements of a Ph.D. in philosophy at Columbia University. The monograph was on the history of microcosmic theories in Western philosophy. At that time he summed up the chances for the future of theories comparing the universe outside to the world within. Microcosmic theories, Conger wrote, are

> philosophical perennials [that] decline when the problem of knowledge is made a difficulty, as well as when interest in the supernatural on the one hand or the humanistic on the other upsets the balance between a consideration more evenly divided between man and the universe; and the theories are likely to be suspected or forgotten in a period when the data of the sciences accumulate faster than they can be organized.

At the time, the appearance of an evolutionary microcosmic theory

> [did] not seem very likely, because the prestige of the natural sciences is now so overwhelming; but if the time ever comes it is possible that the successive complicated repetitions of pattern according to some microcosmic theory may, like the chords of a Pythagorean lyre, or the recurrent motif of a Schopenhauerian symphony, appeal to imaginations eager to catch a strain of what the ancients felt to be the cosmic harmonies. This is, as was said, a field practically unexplored; but certainly somewhere in it there is something which has gone out of the modern world. [4]

In the half century since this was written we recognize that the time is now ripe for a microcosmic evolutionary theory of the universe. Individually, each (wo)man is a mirror of the cell, as the cell in its unity reflects the autopoiesis, the "self-bringing forth" of the planet. Not only (wo)man but also the biosphere is a mirror of the universe. The mirror reflects and it enfolds its own frame: its *rim*. All science to the contrary, we cannot get beyond, we cannot escape this rim. This rim is the edge of the biosphere. We cannot hop over, duck under, or jump beyond this moving ledge; we cannot, as Nietzsche once said, look around our own corner. In sickness and in health, for better or for worse, we are stuck inside the biosphere. We are, and will forever be, with the Earth. Even in space there is no escape from Earth. In space we look back to see the Earth from whence we have come. And yet the Earth has come with us. In the mirror of space there is a face and this face is the biosphere. We recognize it as our own without yet knowing who we are. We still do not know what the Earth is. We do not know who we are. But we do know now that we are inseparable from Earth. Humankind and biosphere are to be married, until extinction do we part. And, like the male partner of a more mundane marriage, we humans, despite our relative youth, will be the first to pass away.

The ancients looked up and saw in the night skies signs of a "large man." This was not just a passing metaphor but a whole microcosmic theory of a correspondence between the little world of the human individual and the great one of the universe that encompassed him. Looking forward, it is possible to imagine a scenario in which the cosmos becomes animated in a way our intellectual forerunners and midnight star-gazers may never have imagined: if life continues to unfold "fractally" in the direction set down here—with individuality reestablishing itself at ever greater levels—biospheres will till the virgin soil of space itself, turning the cosmos into a cosmic garden, and a jungle. And yet that suggests the universe is already always undetached from you. Death becomes—death already always is—the illusion of life's absence. Our destiny is to traverse the universe—and that is exactly what we are doing, right now.

We should have had an inkling something like this would happen.

For life is a wave, and the more it changes, the more it stays the same.

NOTES AND REFERENCES

Introduction

Blanchot epigraph: From Maurice Blanchot, "Literature and the Right to Death," in *The Gaze of Orpheus and Other Literary Essays*, trans. Lydia Davis, ed. P. Adams Sitney (Barrytown, New York: Station Hill Press, 1981), 46.

1. James Lovelock, *Gaia: A New Look at Life on Earth* (New York: Oxford University Press, 1979).
2. J. Allen and M. Nelson, "Space Biospheres," in *The Biosphere Catalogue*, ed. T. P. Snyder (Fort Worth, Texas: Synergetic Press, 1985), 135–137.
3. Quoted in Agnes Arber, *The Mind and the Eye* (Cambridge, England: Cambridge University Press, 1964), 51.
4. Committee on Planetary Biology, Space Science Board, Commission on Physical Sciences, Mathematics, and Resources, National Research Council, *Remote Sensing of the Biosphere* (Washington, D.C.: National Academy Press, 1986), 1.
5. The National Commission on Space, *Pioneering the Space Frontier* (New York: Bantam Books, 1986), 70.
6. Dorion Sagan, "Biosphere II: Meeting Ground for Ecology and Technology," *The Environmentalist* (1987) 7(4):269–278.
7. B. Ivanov and O. Zubareva, "To Mars and Back Again on Board," *Soviet Life* (April 1985):22–25.
8. Clair Folsome, "Microbes," in *The Biosphere Catalogue*, ed. T. P. Snyder (Fort Worth, Texas: Synergetic Press, 1985), 51–56.

9. Dorion Sagan and Lynn Margulis, "Gaia and Biospheres," in *Gaia, the Thesis, the Mechanisms and the Implications: Proceedings of the First Annual Camelford Conference on the Implications of the Gaia Hypothesis,* ed. Peter Bunyard and Edward Goldsmith (Camelford, Cornwall, England: Wadebridge Ecological Centre, Worthyvale Manor, 1988), 237–242.

10. Garrett Hardin and J. Baden, *Managing of the Commons* (San Francisco: W. H. Freeman, 1977).

11. "The CO_2/People Connection," *Science News* (September 12, 1987) 132(11):168.

12. Ilkka Hanski, "Are the Pyramids Deified Dung Pats?" *Ecology and Evolution* (Cambridge: Elsevier, 1988), 34.

Chapter 1

Thoreau epigraph: Quoted in Frederick Turner, *Natural Classicism* (New York: Paragon House, 1985), 178. For context see Thoreau, *Walden* (Merrill Edition, 1969), 98.

1. For the origin of the redwood tree analogy, see James Lovelock, "Gaia: The World as Living Organism," *New Scientist* (December 1986) 18:25–28.

2. For more on the metaphysics of Gaia, see Dorion Sagan, "What Narcissus Saw: The Oceanic Eye," in *The Reality Club 1*, ed. John Brockman (New York: Lynx Books, 1988), 193–214.

3. For a detailed exposition of how the global pollution and poisons of ancient communities of crowded bacteria are a prerequisite to all human metabolism, see Lynn Margulis and Dorion Sagan, *Microcosmos, Four Billion Years of Microbial Evolution* (New York: Summit Books, 1986), especially chap. 6, "The Oxygen Holocaust," pp. 99–114.

4. Peter A. Corning, *The Synergism Hypothesis: A Theory of Progressive Evolution* (New York: McGraw-Hill, 1983), 492 pp.

5. Cited in Frank White, *The Overview Effect: Space Exploration and Human Evolution* (Boston: Houghton Mifflin, 1987), 206.

6. David Abram, "Merleau-Ponty and the Voice of the Earth," Presented as a lecture at the annual gathering of the Merleau-Ponty Circle, New School for Social Research, New York, 1983.

7. Ibid.

Chapter 2

Rumi epigraph: From *Parabola, the Magazine of Myth and Tradition* (Spring 1988):136.

1. Andrey Vitalyevich Lapo, *Traces of Bygone Biospheres* (Moscow: Mir Publishers, 1982), 58. (Revised from 1979 Russian edition.)
2. Cited in ibid., 34.

Chapter 3

1. A short description of Hanson's work may be found in T. P. Snyder, ed., *The Biosphere Catalogue* (Fort Worth, Texas: Synergetic Press, 1985), 178.
2. Cited in Frank White, *The Overview Effect: Space Exploration and Human Evolution* (Boston: Houghton Mifflin, 1987), 206.
3. Vladimir Vernadsky's definition of biosphere is in M. M. Kamshilov, *Evolution of the Biosphere* (Moscow: Mir Publishers, 1976), 78. (English translation.)
4. Cited in Andrey Vitalyevich Lapo, *Traces of Bygone Biospheres* (Moscow: Mir Publishers, 1982), 18. (Revised from 1979 Russian edition.)
5. Cited in R. K. Balandin, *Vladimir Vernadsky*, trans. Alexander Repyev (Moscow: Mir Publishers, 1982), 25.
6. Ibid., 47–48.
7. Vladimir Vernadsky, *The Biosphere* (Oracle, Arizona: Synergetic Press, 1986), 8. (Abridged version based on 1929 French edition.)
8. Ibid., 103. Vernadsky may have borrowed this phrase from English clergyman and chemist Joseph Priestly (1773–1804) or from French chemist Antoine Laurent Lavoisier (1743–1794).
9. Vernadsky's two biospheric principles can be found in Andrey Vitalyevich Lapo, *Traces of Bygone Biospheres* (Moscow: Mir Publishers, 1982), 82–83, as well as in Vernadsky's *The Biosphere*, an abridged version based on the French edition (London: Synergetic Press, 1986), 79–80.
10. For Vernadsky on the "Whole" see Vladimir I. Vernadsky, *Geochimie* (Leipzig: Akademische Verlagsgesellschaft, 1930), 370 pp. Quoted in Jacques Grinevald, "Sketch for a History of the Idea of the Biosphere," Presented at the International Symposium on Gaia, Theory, Practice, and Implications, organized by the Wadebridge Ecological Centre and ECORPA at the Worthyvale Manor Conference Center, Camelford, Cornwall, England, October 21–27, 1987.
11. *Encyclopaedia Britannica* (1984) 10:893–911.
12. Alan Watts, *The Book: On the Taboo Against Knowing Who You Are* (New York: Pantheon, 1966), 89. The "full" citation runs: "Lack of knowl-

edge about the evolution of the organic from the 'inorganic,' coupled with misleading myths about life coming 'into' this world from somewhere 'outside,' has made it difficult for us to see that the biosphere arises, or goes with, a certain degree of geological and astronomical evolution. But, as Douglas E. Harding has pointed out, we tend to think of this planet as life-infested rock, which is as absurd as thinking of the body as a cell-infested skeleton. Surely all forms of life, including man, must be understood as 'symptoms' of the earth, the solar system, and the galaxy—in which case we cannot escape the conclusion that the galaxy is intelligent."

13. Cited in ibid., 97. Original source: Erwin Schrödinger, *My View of the World* (Cambridge, England: Cambridge University Press, 1964), 22.

14. The Vernadsky swarm-of-locusts quote comes from Vernadsky's *Works*, Vol. 4, Book 1, p. 92; it is cited in Andrey Vitalyevich Lapo, *Traces of Bygone Biospheres* (Moscow: Mir Publishers, 1982), 54.

15. Ibid.

16. G. T. Carruthers, "Locusts in the Red Sea," *Nature* (1890) 41:153.

Chapter 4

1. Gregory Bateson, *Mind and Nature: A Necessary Unity* (New York: Dutton, 1979).

2. Humberto R. Maturana and Francisco J. Varela, *Autopoiesis and Cognition. The Realization of the Living*, Boston Studies in the Philosophy of Science, Vol. 42 (Boston: D. Reidel Publishing, 1980), 140 pp.

3. Milan Zeleny, "What Is Autopoiesis?" in *Autopoiesis: A Theory of Living Organization*, ed. Milan Zeleny, The North Holland Series in General Systems Research, Series Vol. 3 (New York: Elsevier, 1981), 4–17.

4. Cited in Richard Marshall and Robert Mapplethorpe, *50 New York Artists* (San Francisco: Chronicle Books, 1986).

5. James Hutton, *Theory of the Earth; or an Investigation of the Laws Observable in the Composition, Dissolution, and Restoration of Land upon the Globe*, Transcripts of the Royal Society, Edinburgh, Vol. 1, Pt. 1 (1788), 209–304.

6. Delivered by James Hutton in a 1785 lecture before the Royal Society of Edinburgh. Cited in James Lovelock, "Gaia: An Example of Large-Scale Biological Design," Presented at the 1988 Conference on Biology as a Basis of Design, Perugia, Italy, 1988.

7. James Lovelock, "Geophysiology: The Science of Gaia," Draft of a paper read at the Chapman Conference of the American Geophysical Union, San Diego, March 1988.

8. Ibid.

9. Alfred Lotka, *Physical Biology* (1925), cited in ibid.

10. Martin Heidegger, "The Origin of the Work of Art," in *Poetry, Language, Thought*, trans. Albert Hofstadter (New York: Harper and Row, 1971), 15–88.
11. Nancy Jack Todd and John Todd, *Bioshelters, Ocean Arks, City Farming: Ecology as the Basis of Design* (San Francisco: Sierra Club Books, 1984), 210 pp. I am told that this work is selling very well in Japan, suggesting that, however far-off and dreamy we may consider the notion of engineering urban and marine biospheric ecosystems, the Japanese consider it a viable present reality.

Chapter 5

1. Peter Nicholls, ed., *The Science in Science Fiction* (New York: Knopf, 1983), 208 pp.
2. Robert H. Haynes, "Ecce Ecopoiesis: Playing God on Mars." Haynes is at the Department of Biology, York University, Toronto, Canada. As far as I know, this has not yet been published.
3. James E. Oberg, *New Earths* (Harrisburg, Pennsylvania: Stackpole Books, 1981).
4. Lynn Margulis and Karlene Schwartz, *Five Kingdoms: An Illustrated Guide to the Phyla of Life on Earth* (New York: W. H. Freeman, 1988). The five-kingdom hand I designed adorns the cover of the second edition and can be found as the frontispiece to the first edition.
5. For more on camel recycling and nonhuman engineering, see Bernhardt Lotsch, *Man, Earth, and the Challenges* (Santa Fe, New Mexico: Synergetic Press, 1981), 92–111.
6. Clair Folsome, "Microbes," in *The Biosphere Catalogue*, ed. T. P. Snyder (Fort Worth, Texas: Synergetic Press, 1985), 51–56.
7. Herbert Spencer, *The Principles of Sociology*, 3 vols., 3d ed. (New York: Appleton, 1897), 1:592; cited in Peter Corning, *The Synergism Hypothesis* (New York: McGraw-Hill, 1983), 209.
8. Arthur Koestler, *Janus: A Summing Up* (Picador, London: Pan Books, 1978). For a good summary on the need for multiple levels of individuality in evolutionary theory see N. Eldredge and S. N. Salthe, "Hierarchy and Evolution," *Oxford Surveys in Evolutionary Biology*, Vol. 1, ed. R. Dawkins and M. Ridley (New York: Oxford University Press, 1984), 184–208.

Chapter 6

1. James Lovelock, *Ages of Gaia: A Biography of Our Living Earth* (New York: Norton, 1988), 226.
2. From the television program "Goddess of the Earth," *Nova*, Transcript

no. 1302, originally broadcast on PBS, January 28, 1986, WGBH Educational Foundation.

Chapter 7

1. Gwynne Dyer, *The Toronto Star* (1988).
2. Cited in Joseph Campbell, *The Way of Animal Powers*, Vol. 1, *Historical Atlas of World Mythology* (San Francisco: Harper and Row, 1983), 251.
3. Frank White, *The Overview Effect: Space Exploration and Human Evolution* (Boston: Houghton Mifflin, 1987), 318 pp.
4. See, for example, James Lovelock, "Geophysiology: A New Look at Earth Science," *Bulletin of the American Meterological Society*, (April 1986) 67(4):392–397. For a less technical treatment, see James Lovelock, "Gaia: The World as a Living Organism," *New Scientist* (December 1986):25–28.
5. For more on the links, or lack thereof, between plankton and the biosphere, see Richard Monastersky, "The Plankton-Climate Connection," *Science News* (December 5, 1987) 132(23):362–365.
6. Stephen E. Schwartz, "Are Global Cloud Albedo and Climate Controlled by Marine Phytoplankton?" *Nature* (December 1988) 336(1):441–445.
7. James Lovelock, *Ages of Gaia. A Biography of Our Living Earth* (New York: Norton, 1988), 105.
8. Peter Russell, *The Global Brain* (Los Angeles: J. P. Tarcher, 1983), 82.
9. Lewis Thomas, "Beyond the Moon's Horizon—Our Home," *The New York Times* (July 15, 1989):25.

Chapter 8

1. Ludwig Fleck, *Genesis and Development of a Scientific Fact*, Thaddeus J. Trenn and Robert K. Merton, eds. (Chicago: University of Chicago Press, 1979). It is very difficult to finish this book and still cling to the notion of a scientific reality independent of the human society that manufactures it.
2. François Jacob, *The Possible and the Actual* (New York: Pantheon, 1982). The Foucault quote, from *Le Monde*, is reprinted on the back cover.
3. David Abram, "Merleau-Ponty and the Voice of the Earth," Presented as a lecture at the annual gathering of the Merleau-Ponty Circle, New School for Social Research, New York, 1983.
4. Cited in ibid.
5. Cited in Dorion Sagan, ed., *The Global Sulfur Cycle*, NASA Technical Memorandum 87570 (Washington, D.C., 1985), 241.
6. The full Freud quote runs: "The ego . . . plays the ridiculous role of the clown in the circus whose gestures are intended to persuade the audience

that all the changes on the stage are brought about by his orders. But only the youngest members of the audience are taken in by him." From *History of the Psychoanalytic Movement*, p. 97; cited in Walter Kaufmann, *Discovering the Mind*, Vol. 3, *Freud versus Adler and Jung* (New York: McGraw-Hill, 1980), 467.

Chapter 9

Bruno epigraph: From Wolfgang E. Drumbein and Betsey Dexter Dyer, "This Planet Is Alive: Weathering and Biology, a Multi-Faceted Problem," in *The Chemistry of Weathering*, ed. J. I. Drever (Boston: D. Reidel Publishing, 1985), 145.

Butler epigraph: From Samuel Butler, "The Book of Machines," in *Erewhon or, Over the Range*; quoted in Laurence Behrens and Leonard J. Rosen, *Themes and Variations: The Impact of Great Ideas* (Glenview, Illinois: Scott Foresman/ Little, Brown College Division, 1988), 482–490.

1. Bernard Campbell, *Human Ecology: The Story of Our Place in Nature from Prehistory to the Present* (New York: Aldine, 1985), 190.
2. For Wilson's broadening of the concept of sociobiological genetic selfishness to include larger collectives and, indeed, all of life, see E. O. Wilson, "Sociobiology: From Darwin to the Present, in *Darwin's Legacy*, ed. Charles L. Hamrum, Nobel Conference 18 (San Francisco: Harper and Row, 1983), 53–75.
3. E. O. Wilson, *Biophilia: The Human Bond with Other Species* (Cambridge: Harvard University Press, 1984), 157 pp.

Chapter 10

1. For more on Calhoun, see Bruce Bower, "Population Overload: Mice Advice," *Science News* (May 1986) 129(22):346–347. Also David P. Barash, *The Hare and the Tortoise: Culture, Biology, and Human Nature* (New York: Penguin, 1986), 231–233, 283.
2. For a comparison of Earth's Archean-Proterozoic transition to puberty, see James Lovelock, *Ages of Gaia: A Biography of Our Living Earth* (New York: Norton, 1988), 99.
3. Samuel Butler, "The Book of Machines," in *Erewhon or, Over the Range*; quoted in Laurence Behrens and Leonard J. Rosen, *Themes and Variations: The Impact of Great Ideas* (Glenview, Illinois: Scott Foresman/Little, Brown College Division, 1988), 482–490.

Chapter 11

1. All of the following Butler quotes may be found in the collected works. See especially Samuel Butler, *The Works of Samuel Butler*, Vol. 20, Note-Books (New York: AMS Press, 1968).
2. Bruce Bower, "Retooled Ancestors," *Science News* (May 28, 1988) 133(22):344–345.
3. William Calvin, *The Throwing Madonna: Essays on the Brain* (New York: McGraw-Hill, 1983), 253 pp.
4. Marshall McLuhan, *Understanding Media* (New York: McGraw-Hill, 1966), 66.

Chapter 12

1. Norman Myers, "The Extinction Spasm Impending: Synergisms at Work," *Conservation Biology* (May 1987) 1(1):14–21.
2. James Lovelock, "Geophysiology: A New Look at Earth Science," *Bulletin of the American Meteorological Society* (April 1986) 67(4):392–397.
3. M. M. Kamshilov, *Evolution of the Biosphere* (Moscow: Mir Publishers, 1976), 91–93. Original experiments described in M. M. Kamshilov, "The Buffer Action of a Biological System," *Zhurnal Obshchei Biologii* (1973) 34(2). (In Russian.)

Chapter 13

1. Cited in Robert Wright, *Three Scientists and Their Gods: Looking for Meaning in an Age of Information* (New York: Times Books, 1988), 222.

Chapter 14

1. Ian McHarg, *Design with Nature* (New York: Doubleday, 1967), 43–54.
2. B. Ivanov and O. Zubareva, "To Mars and Back Again on Board," *Soviet Life* (April 1985):22–25.
3. Dorion Sagan, "Biosphere II: Meeting Ground for Ecology and Technology," *The Environmentalist* (1987) 7(4):271–281.
4. "Biosphere Test Begins, Biologist to Live for Five Days in Sealed Module," *Daily Hampshire Gazette*, Northampton, Massachusetts (March 9, 1989).
5. Cited in Frederick Turner, *Natural Classicism: Essays on Literature and Science* (New York: Paragon House, 1985).

Chapter 15

1. Cited in Benoit Mandelbrot, *The Fractal Geometry of Nature* (New York: W. H. Freeman, 1977), 419.
2. Gottfried Leibniz, *Monadology and Other Philosophical Essays*, trans. Paul Schrecker and Anne Martin Schrecker, (Indianapolis: Bobbs-Merrill, 1965), 156–157.
3. The quote and the example come from David Bohm, *Wholeness and the Implicate Order* (New York: Routledge and Kegan Paul, 1980).
4. George Perrigo Conger, *Theories of Macrocosms and Microcosms in the History of Philosophy* (New York: Columbia University Press, 1922), 136.

INDEX